Cambridge Elements

Elements in Publishing and Book Culture
edited by
Samantha Rayner
University College London
Rebecca Lyons
University of Bristol

THE FOREVER FANDOM OF HARRY POTTER

Balancing Fan Agency and Corporate Control

Marianne Martens
Kent State University, Ohio

CAMBRIDGE
UNIVERSITY PRESS

University Printing House, Cambridge CB2 8BS, United Kingdom

One Liberty Plaza, 20th Floor, New York, NY 10006, USA

477 Williamstown Road, Port Melbourne, VIC 3207, Australia

314–321, 3rd Floor, Plot 3, Splendor Forum, Jasola District Centre,
New Delhi – 110025, India

79 Anson Road, #06–04/06, Singapore 079906

Cambridge University Press is part of the University of Cambridge.

It furthers the University's mission by disseminating knowledge in the pursuit of
education, learning, and research at the highest international levels of excellence.

www.cambridge.org
Information on this title: www.cambridge.org/9781108469883
DOI: 10.1017/9781108599092

First published 2019

A catalogue record for this publication is available from the British Library.

ISBN 978-1-108-46988-3 Paperback
ISSN 2514-8524 (online)
ISSN 2514-8516 (print)

The Forever Fandom of Harry Potter

Balancing Fan Agency and Corporate Control

Elements in Publishing and Book Culture

DOI: 10.1017/9781108599092

First published online: June 2019

Marianne Martens

Kent State University, Ohio

Author for correspondence: Marianne Martens, mmarten3@kent.edu

ABSTRACT: Harry Potter fans contribute their immaterial and affective labor in multiple arenas: as peer-to-peer marketers via fan sites and social media; as participants in amateur fan festivals; or as activists for social change. Fans' participation in the Harry Potter universe has contributed to its success. This Element examines how fans' labor might continue to support the franchise for future readers. Starting with the context and theoretical frameworks that support a multidimensional analysis of the Harry Potter fan experience, this Element examines tensions between fans and Warner Bros., as fan participation tests the limits of corporate control.

KEYWORDS: affective and immaterial labor, celebrity authorship, media and culture, young adult literature, fandom and pop culture

ISBNs: 9781108469883 (PB), 9781108599092 (OC)

ISSNs: 2514-8524 (online), 2514-8516 (print)

Contents

Introduction

In my book *Publishers, Readers, and Digital Engagement*,[1] I explored how young people participate in book-related sites online – from participatory book-reviewing sites such as Random Buzzers; to fan sites such as Twilight Saga; to a co-created series such as The Amanda Project, in which the publisher asked readers to contribute storylines for forthcoming books in the series – and how in turn these processes commodify young people. This Element starts where that book ended, and focuses on the complex relationship between fans and the "owners" of their fandom: in this case, examining *Harry Potter* fans across transmedia landscapes, and their relationships with the rights holders, J. K. Rowling and Warner Bros. Ownership in this context becomes an encumbered term. Corporate owners have a very clear idea of ownership, backed up by an established system of copyright law and the financial means to support lawsuits. Fans certainly have their own claims of ownership, and while they may lack financial means to challenge a corporate behemoth such as Warner Bros., as a united fan community[2] they increasingly have the power of social media platforms to influence decisions. When conflicts arise, each side has much to lose.

Genre is both a construct and a marketing tool. In children's literature, genre boundaries are connected to developmental stages, and to children's stages in school, but are also governed by markets and salability. For example, after the publication of S. E. Hinton's (1967) book *The Outsiders*, generally recognized as the first work of young adult (YA) fiction published in the United States, YA quickly became a burgeoning genre of "realist fiction" that was closely tied to social change, covering issues such as sex, war, and drug abuse.[3] Thirty years later, J. K. Rowling's *Harry Potter* series was a genre-pushing series, elevating the "fantasy" genre to prominence for those who read the books. Within the overarching genre of

---

[1] M. Martens, *Publishers, Readers, and Digital Engagement* (London: Palgrave Macmillan, 2016).

[2] H. Jenkins, *Textual Poachers: Television Fans and Participatory Culture* (New York: Routledge, 2012).

[3] Martens, *Publishers*.

children's literature, fantasy is a sub-genre with especially fluid boundaries. The *Harry Potter* books are crossover titles, which means that even though they were initially published as books for young people, their appeal extends across a wide demographic. Arguably, *Harry Potter* was a genre-busting series, with the books behaving more like works of adult fiction than like books published for young readers. Beginning with *Harry Potter and the Philosopher's Stone* in 1997 in the United Kingdom (and in 1998 in the United States, where it was published as *Harry Potter and the Sorcerer's Stone*), J. K. Rowling's *Harry Potter* books changed the publishing landscape for young people in terms of sales figures, best-seller status, and book length, from the first book's appearance in 1997 to the last in 2007. The first book spent 442 weeks on the *New York Times* best-seller list, and as of September 2017, it was the fifth most read book on Amazon.com.[4] In fact, the series prompted the need for a separate children's best-seller list at the *New York Times* because it constantly took over the first four entries on the combined list, and subsequently created a need for a separate children's "series" list.[5] As a crossover series, it appeals to a demographic beyond its original intended audience of children, and, with over 500 million copies sold, it is the best-selling series of all time.[6] The individual books have topped best-selling books lists such as a 2016 one by *The Guardian* Data Blog, on which the seven Harry Potter books hold places in the top ten spots, with three spots lost to the following "adult" titles: no. 1, *The DaVinci Code* by Dan Brown, no. 5, *Fifty Shades of Grey* by E. L. James,

[4] *New York Times*, "Children's series," September 24, 2017, www.nytimes.com /books/best-sellers/2017/09/24/series-books/?action=click&contentColl ection=Books&referrer=https%3A%2F%2Fwww.google.com%2F&region= Header&module=ArrowNav&version=Right&pgtype=Reference

[5] D. Garner, "Ten years later, Harry Potter vanishes from the best-seller list," *New York Times*, May 1, 2008, https://artsbeat.blogs.nytimes.com/2008/05/01/ ten-years-later-harry-potter-vanishes-from-the-best-seller-list/?mcubz=3&_r=0

[6] J. Weiss, "Harry Potter becomes best-selling book series in history with more than 500 million copies sold worldwide," *Syfy Wire*, February 2, 2018, www .syfy.com/syfywire/harry-potter-becomes-best-selling-book-series-in-history-with-more-than-500-million-copies

and no. 9, *Angels and Demons* by Dan Brown.[7] Adding pirated copies and books that have been shared, either via libraries or between readers, to the number of sold books means that *Harry Potter* is probably the most read series of all time. Nicolette Jones, the children's books editor of the London *Sunday Times*, noted that *Harry Potter*'s impact on literature and the cultural consciousness has been pervasive.[8] Even our language has changed, with words from the book, such as "muggle," added to the *Oxford English Dictionary*. Before J. K. Rowling, the best-selling children's author in the United Kingdom was Enid Blyton, who died in 1968. Blyton was well known for many series including *The Famous Five* and *The Secret Seven*.[9] Yet by 2016, while the *Harry Potter* books took up top ten slots in *The Guardian*'s Data Blog, books by Enid Blyton did not appear on the list.

The Harry Potter series coincided with a boom in Internet use. FanFiction.net started in October 1998, which was fortuitous timing, as *Harry Potter* was the perfect vehicle for online fandom. Websites independently made by young fans served as the best kind of peer-to-peer marketing for the books initially, and later for the movies as well. According to Murray, "the first Harry Potter book had built its audience through extensive word-of-mouth in Internet-enabled forums such as chat rooms and electronic message boards rather than through corporate-coordinated publicity."[10] These were the ur–fan sites, later replaced by professional and corporate-owned sites, as we will see herein.

As a contemporary blockbuster appealing to boys and girls, children and adults, *Harry Potter* is the ultimate transmedia property. Twenty years after

---

[7] DataBlog, "The top 100 bestselling books of all time: How does Fifty Shades of Grey compare?" *The Guardian*, August 9, 2012, www.theguardian.com/news/datablog/2012/aug/09/best-selling-books-all-time-fifty-shades-grey-compare

[8] N. Jones, "The Harry Potter effect: A discussion on how the Harry Potter books have changed the landscape of children's literature and permeated our cultural consciousness," *Royal Society of Literature*, November 23, 2017, https://rsliterature.org/library-article/the-harry-potter-effect/

[9] Jones, "Harry Potter effect."

[10] S. Murray, "'Celebrating the story the way it is': Cultural studies, corporate media and the contested utility of fandom," *Continuum*, 18 (2004), 16.

the first book's initial publication, *Harry Potter's* segment of the entertainment marketplace remains significant, as it spans multiple media platforms: books, film, theater, licensed merchandise, an amusement park, festivals, a play, a movie-studio/museum, a traveling exhibition originating at the British Library, and academic work including university courses, publications, and conferences. Because of the world-building within the series, *Harry Potter* lends itself to fan participation on a large scale, and its audience is active like no other.

Harry Potter's appeal stretches across a wide demographic, from newly-reading children to adults, in part because Harry and his friends grow up over the course of the series. For some early readers, reading a *Harry Potter* book is a sign of accomplishment – a proudly carried badge of literacy. Ebooks allow adult fans to read the books privately, without having to be embarrassed about visibly reading "children's" literature. The first readers of the books, who grew up experiencing the publication of nearly a book a year, matured along with the characters. This sets the series apart from other popular series – such as the Stratemeyer Syndicate's *Nancy Drew* mystery stories, in which Nancy Drew ages only two years during the series' entire seventy-four-year course – which tend to be read by a specific demographic of reader in terms of age and gender. In the first book, Harry is an eleven-year-old child; the series follows him through his childhood and teen years, and then concludes with an epilogue featuring adult Harry with children of his own. While many readers were able to grow up along with Harry, the epilogue is much contested. According to Lesley Goodman, some fans "considered it a betrayal of the fictional universe that the only details important enough to appear in the epilogue are marriages and children," and indeed, the epilogue primarily describes marriages between Harry and Ginny, Ron and Hermione, and what they named their children.[11] Further, "while many fans have defended the epilogue against these charges, explaining why it did not fail the fictional universe, rejecting the epilogue has

[11] L. Goodman, "Disappointing fans: Fandom, fictional theory, and the death of the author," *Journal of Popular Culture*, 48 (2015), 670.

nonetheless created an entire genre of Harry Potter fan fiction, labeled EWE: 'Epilogue, What Epilogue?'"[12]

Another reason for the wide readership is the rich world-building that exists within the books, which makes the series appealing to virtually any reader. This world-building also lends itself exceptionally well to fandoms and fan fiction – and, as we will see later, a complicated relationship between owners and fans. Whether it is magic, orphans, or the classic battle of good versus evil, there is something in the series for nearly everyone, and arguably it is not just the world-building that gives the *Harry Potter* story longevity.

Harry Potter fan studies are situated in a larger realm of fan scholarship and, like the fandom itself, exist across a large ecology of activity – from fan fiction, to participating in festivals, to political activism (in the name of Harry). The balancing of fan agency with corporate control has been explored before, as in television-based fan studies by Henry Jenkins[13] or Camille Bacon-Smith,[14] or Jenkins' *Convergence Culture*,[15] in which he explores what happens when analog media formats collide with new online participatory opportunities. While active audiences existed pre-Internet – for example, Tilley[16] describes how twentieth-century comic fans wrote to comic creators to suggest storylines and criticize content, and Pearson describes angry fans engaged in letter writing when *Star Trek* creator Rod Serling canceled the series in 1962[17] – online active audiences are far easier to see, track, study, and engage.

According to Plante, Roberts, Reysen, and Gerbasi, belonging to fan culture "can have a potentially deep and meaningful impact on our values,

[12] Ibid. [13] Jenkins, *Textual Poachers*.

[14] C. Bacon-Smith, *Enterprising Women: Television Fandom and the Creation of the Popular Myth* (Philadelphia: University of Pennsylvania Press, 1992).

[15] H. Jenkins, *Convergence Culture* (New York: New York University Press, 2008).

[16] C. Tilley, "Children and comics: Young readers take on the critics." In J. P. Danky and J. L. Baughman, eds., *Protest on the Pages: Essays on Print and the Culture of Dissent since 1865* (Madison, WI: University of Wisconsin Press, 2015).

[17] R. Pearson, "Fandom in the digital era," *Popular Communication*, 8 (2010), 84–95.

identity, and potentially, our behavior."[18] According to Tosenberger's definition, fan fiction "utilizes pre-existing characters and settings from a literary or media text," and the world built by Rowling provides endless opportunities for expansion.[19] The *Star Wars* series is one of similar scale in terms of world-building, transmedia, and fan participation, and it also has multiple similarities in terms of content – something which has not escaped fan attention. A Google search for 'Harry Potter versus Star Wars' brings up an abundance of both fan-created and professional content comparing plot similarities between the two franchises: from YouTube videos, to memes, to blog postings. A SparkNotes blog post by Maddy Aaron interprets plot elements of the *Star Wars* movies through a *Harry Potter* lens.[20] Another blog post on the Digital Spy site argues that the *Star Wars* and *Harry Potter* plots are identical, starting with "orphan[s] fighting evil with pointy sticks."[21]

Indeed, the books follow in a long tradition of children's literature in which children successfully act on their own – without parental intervention. Such children abound across Western children's literature: Astrid Lindgren's *Pippi Longstocking*, Roald Dahl's *James and the Giant Peach*, C. S. Lewis's *Narnia* books, Philip Pullman's *His Dark Materials* trilogy, and Lemony Snicket's *A Series of Unfortunate Events* collection. Indeed, in the classic stories, from "Cinderella" to *The Wonderful Wizard of Oz*, the hero's parents are more likely to be absent or dead than cruel or incompetent. In fact, it's the removal of the adults' protective presence that kickstarts

---

[18] C. N. Plante, S. E. Roberts, S. Reysen, and K. C. Gerbasi, "'One of us': Engagement with fandoms and global citizenship identification," *Psychology of Popular Media Culture*, 3 (2014), 61.

[19] C. Tosenberger, "Homosexuality at the online Hogwarts: Harry Potter slash fanfiction," *Children's Literature*, 36 (2008), 185.

[20] M. Aaron, "So you haven't seen *Star Wars* . . . A *Harry Potter* geek's guide to a galaxy far, far away," November 10, 2015, http://community.sparknotes.com /2015/11/10/so-you-havent-seen-star-wars-a-harry

[21] M. Hill, "16 reasons why Star Wars and Harry Potter are secretly EXACTLY the same: May the 'orphan fighting evil with magic pointy sticks' be with you," *Digital Spy*, January 12, 2016, www.digitalspy.com/movies/star-wars/feature/ a779720/16-reasons

the story, so the orphan can begin her or his "triumphant rise."[22] This aligns also with Vladimir Propp's functions of dramatis personae, specifically, function no. 1: "One of the members of a family absents himself from home." Propp explains that such absences can occur with a parent leaving home (for example, to go to work) or the death of a parent, or when the younger person "absents" him- or herself.[23]

The character of Holden Caulfield in J. D. Salinger's 1951 *The Catcher in the Rye* provides another example, and that book was published as adult fiction despite its young protagonist. In the *Harry Potter* series, courageous acts are generally based on Harry and his friends subverting adult authority and breaking rules, whether it is Harry illegally using magic at the Dursleys' home or the trio of Harry, Ron, and Hermione sneaking around Hogwarts at night, often in areas whose names forbid entry, such as the "Forbidden Forest" or the "Restricted Section" of the library.

Since *Harry Potter*, there have been other blockbuster series for young people – notably the *Twilight* series by Stephenie Meyer (the last book, *Breaking Dawn*, was published in 2008) or the *Hunger Games* trilogy by Suzanne Collins (the last of which was published in 2010). In recent years, online fandoms for young people have greatly proliferated. Digital tools have blurred lines in the field between "authors," "readers," and "publishers,"[24] which means that authors now have to market their own works:[24] they now have an intrinsic role in connecting with and maintaining relationships with fans by using social media to generate and build fan support for their own works. The most successful YA titles quickly transition to multiple platforms and are optioned for film or television. For example, Maggie Stiefvater, author of the best-selling series *The Raven Cycle*, which as of this writing is being made into a television series, is very active on multiple social media platforms, and even provides a guide for fans on where to find

---

[22] J. Just, "The parent problem in young adult lit," *New York Times*, April 1, 2010, www.nytimes.com/2010/04/04/books/review/Just-t.html?pagewanted=all

[23] V. Propp, *Morphology of the Folktale*, 2nd edn. (Austin, TX, and London: University of Texas Press, 1968), 26.

[24] See Martens, *Publishers* for an in-depth discussion.

her online.[25] Another blockbuster YA author, John Green (author of *The Fault in Our Stars*, 2012), is well known as a YouTube star of videos in which he and his brother Hank Green post as the Vlogbrothers.[26] They also have an educational YouTube series called Crash Course.[27] Stiefvater and Green's efforts serve to keep fans engaged in between book releases. Among these online communities, *Harry Potter* fans may well be the most numerous, the most varied, and the most loyal to a series. In order to compare *Harry Potter* with other recent YA blockbusters, a comparison chart of activity across Fanfiction.net, Archive of Our Own, Reddit, and Twitter is shown in Table 1.

In each case, the *Harry Potter* series attracts more fans and activity. Typically, fandoms around blockbuster series run their course. Even the enormous fandom around the *Twilight Saga* has faded, and Hachette's *Twilight Saga* site[28] now exists mostly as an extended advertisement for the series. But *Harry Potter* fandom continues strong, more than twenty years after publication of the first book in the series.

Rowling's rich world-building within the series creates seemingly endless opportunities for transmedia experiences – and for multi-dimensional academic analysis such as I undertake here. As the last book in the series was published in 2007, aging *Harry Potter* fans lend a new dimension to the study as well. As evidenced by the sites explored herein, *Harry Potter* fan culture is a way of life. In analyzing the multiple dimensions of *Harry Potter* fandom, this Element takes a holistic look at the participatory culture of the *Harry Potter* fandom experience, exploring three interconnected arenas: (1) online fan sites and social media extensions thereof; (2) unofficial, unauthorized Harry Potter festivals; and (3) fan activism.[29] Together, these discussions examine fans' participation, from the digital world to the physical world and

---

[25] M. Stiefvater, "About," Tumblr, 2018, http://maggie-stiefvater.tumblr.com /about

[26] Vlogbrothers [podcast], "Featured," YouTube, n.d., www.youtube.com/user/ vlogbrothers/featured

[27] J. Green et al. "About," *Crash Course*, n.d., https://thecrashcourse.com/about

[28] www.thetwilightsaga.com/   [29] Jenkins, *Textual Poachers*.

Table 1 Comparative fan engagement across multiple series (2018)

	Harry Potter	Twilight	Hunger Games
Fanfiction.net: book community and forums	8,727 communities 1,685 forums	3,917 communities 702 forums	231 communities 374 forums
Archive of Our Own: fan fics	192,248	13,104	11,320
Reddit	r/harrypotter 530,000 members www.reddit.com/r/harry potter/wiki/ megathread	r/twilight 2,400 members www.reddit.com/r/ twilight	r/hungergames 18,200 members www.reddit.com/r/ hungergames
Official author's Twitter account and number of followers	https://twitter.com /jk_rowling? ref_src=twsrc% 5Egoogle%7Ctwcamp% 5Eserp%7Ctwgr% 5Eauthor 14,500,000 @jkrowling	https://twitter.com /_StephenieMeyer? lang=en* 8,416 @_StephenieMeyer *Deactivated in 2010	No official Twitter account

back, and at the same time reveal the delicate balance between fans and corporations, both of whom are deeply invested in the franchise.

My methods are qualitative and include the following techniques:

(1) observations (online and face-to-face) of fan sites and festivals;
(2) interviews with fans, including writers of fan fiction;[30] an organizer of a Potterfest in Kent, Ohio; an organizer of the Harry Potter Festival in Odense, Denmark; an editor of *The Bookseller*, the British trade journal for the publishing industry;[31] the president of Kent State's Harry Potter Alliance (HPA); and a staff member at the HPA's national (US) office;
(3) close readings and content analysis of *Harry Potter*–related social media, including Facebook, Pottermore, PottermoreForum, Reddit, and Twitter;[32] fan sites such as Pottermore; and websites of various Harry Potter festivals, including the Harry Potter Festival Odense;[33]
(4) information provided by Alexa Internet about the "popularity" of fan sites.

In addition, media coverage in newspapers and social media, blogs, and memes from the US and Denmark, as well as articles from the book trade, contributed to the findings herein.

The first section of this Element describes the context and theoretical frameworks that support a multidimensional analysis of the Harry Potter experience, including (1) fan agency, corporate (and fan) ownership, and conflicts with participation; (2) literary celebrity (as Rowling is perhaps the ultimate contemporary literary celebrity); (3) Bourdieu's field theory; (4)

---

[30] K. W., K. E., and O. P. are adult fans interviewed herein.

[31] Her US counterpart at *Publishers Weekly* did not respond to requests for an interview.

[32] For Twitter data, initially, close readings of Twitter following #Pottermore clearly demonstrated fans' displeasure. Later, a colleague, Emad Khazraee, used the Personal Zombie application to search Twitter for #Pottermore. This resulted in a data set of 7,062 tweets between September 14, 2015 and October 2, 2015. Tweets were then categorized around the themes that emerged, and analyzed.

[33] https://magiskedageodense.dk/

the *Harry Potter* fandom community and the symbiotic relationship between the fans and the corporate owners; and, finally, (5) the immaterial and affective labor[34] that is an integral component of fan culture, as fan labor promotes the brand.

Section 2 examines the growth of fan sites as they expanded from tiny, individually created sites to larger participatory sites such as Mugglenet and Wizarding World, and finally Rowling's own Pottermore site. Arguably, Pottermore was inspired by, and built upon, fans' sites. While Rowling and Warner Bros. initially had fraught relationships with fans' online activities (including cease-and-desist letters and lawsuits, as will be discussed later), by 2004, Rowling's personal site, jkrowling.com, had launched the Fan Site Award, acknowledging the value of fans' participation. This award, however, was short-lived. According to Fanlore.org, no award has been given since 2007, which could coincide with the start of the Harry Potter Lexicon trial, and could indicate the beginning of a more complicated relationship between Rowling, Warner Bros., and online fans.[35]

Section 3 examines the phenomenon of Harry Potter festivals as live, affordable fan events that, like the fan sites, test the limits of corporate cooperation, and that exist in the interstices between literary festivals and large-scale pop culture events such as the San Diego Comic-Con and its various corporate-owned spin-offs. Using the 2017 Potterfest in Kent, Ohio, as a case study, and Odense's Harry Potter Festival (now Magiske Dage Odense) as a counterexample, this section studies conflicts between fans, small-scale festival organizers, and Warner Bros., which controls most licensing rights.[36]

---

[34] T. Terranova, "Free labor: Producing culture for the digital economy," *Social Text*, 63 (2000), 33–57.

[35] Fanlore.org, "J. K. Rowling Fan Site Award," 2016, https://fanlore.org/wiki/J.K._Rowling_Fan_Site_Award

[36] A complete discussion of who owns which licensing rights to the *Harry Potter* franchise is beyond the scope of this monograph, but in general terms, Warner Bros. Consumer Products (herein referred to as "Warner Bros.") acquired worldwide licensing rights as part of the movie deal for the books. J. K. Rowling has reserved rights to the books and theatrical rights. For further details on which

Section 4 examines the Harry Potter Alliance as a site that promotes fan activism and organizes good deeds in the name of *Harry Potter*, while connecting fans with a community of like-minded individuals via live and online activities, from boycotts to the Granger Leadership Academy (GLA), where members find empowerment, agency, and the experience of making positive social change, all in the name of Harry – or Hermione.

Now that the canonical *Harry Potter* series (and the films) have been completed, this Element concludes with a discussion of the future of *Harry Potter* fandom. As fans' participation is arguably a big component of the success of the series, will the cocreated (as described later herein) spin-off products, or what Lauren Camacci[37] calls the "para-canon," from the *Fantastic Beast* movies, to Pottermore content, to theatrical plays, be enough to interest, engage, and sustain a new generation of devoted fans, whose participation will contribute to the life (and after-life) of the series? Will J. K. Rowling continue to engage with fans – and with her content – as she revises and modifies the canon online? And how has the series inspired a new generation of activists? Despite struggles between fandom and ownership in the digital realm, within this research, I am interested in how fandom will impact the future of *Harry Potter*, and how fan participation might just be a required element, necessary to keep the series fresh and alive for new generations of readers, despite conflicts with J. K. Rowling and Warner Bros.

1 Context: the Harry Potter Landscape

While reading is generally considered a solitary activity, the *Harry Potter* reading experience includes communal, participatory options. As pop-culture scholar Jim Collins writes, reading, which used to be "a thoroughly private experience in which readers engaged in intimate conversation with

rights are controlled by J. K. Rowling versus those controlled by Warner Bros., see www.jkrowling.com/tcs/

[37] L. Camacci, "What counts as Harry Potter canon?" *In Media Res: A Media Commons Project*, November 10, 2016, http://mediacommons.org/imr/2016/11/10/what-counts-harry-potter-canon

an author between the pages of a book, has become an exuberantly social activity, whether it be in the form of actual book clubs, television book clubs [Oprah], Internet chat rooms, or the entire set of rituals involved in 'going to Barnes & Noble.'"[38] Ironically, less than ten years after the publication of Collins's book, many of the book-related activities he described have already either disappeared or changed significantly. Television book clubs such as Oprah Winfrey's have gone off the air. Internet chat rooms have become fan sites, and Barnes & Noble is no longer a cultural behemoth as it faces competition from online retailers, especially Amazon.com in the US. All of these venues serve as opportunities to extend the *Harry Potter* experience. The sense of community that fans feel in engaging in these activities around a beloved pop culture universe connects them with like-minded individuals and creates virtual and physical friendships.

Popular Culture

In order to define popular culture, it is necessary to examine both "popular" and "culture." According to Raymond Williams, the term "popular" was historically infused with negative connotations about being "low" or "base."[39] But by the early twentieth century, the meaning shifted and began to acquire positive connotations, as culture that is "well-liked by the people."[40] Yet it still bears connotations of inferiority. Williams describes "popular literature," the "popular press," or "popular entertainment" as "work deliberately setting out to win favour with the people," rather than work that is of high quality.[41]

For Williams's student John Fiske, "culture" is about identity and meaning making:

> Culture is the constant process of producing meanings of and
> from our social experience, and such meanings necessarily

---

[38] J. Collins, *Bring on the Books for Everybody: How Literary Culture Became Popular Culture* (Durham, NC: Duke University Press, 2010), 4.

[39] R. Williams, *Keywords: A Vocabulary of Culture and Society*, rev. edn. (New York: Oxford University Press, 1983), 236.

[40] Ibid. [41] Ibid., 237.

> produce a social identity for the people involved. Making sense of anything involves making sense of the person who is the agent in the process; sense making dissolves differences between subject and object and constructs each in relation to the other. Within the production and circulation of these meanings lies pleasure.[42]

Meaning making connects to one's social identity and this is deeply associated with *Harry Potter* fandom, as we will see herein. Moving beyond "culture" and towards "popular culture," Fiske writes that popular culture is about hierarchies: "Popular culture is the culture of the subordinated and disempowered and thus always bears within it signs of power relations, traces of the forces of domination and subordination that are central to our social system and therefore to our social experience. Equally, it shows signs of resisting or evading these forces: popular culture contradicts itself."[43]

In a similar way, one might argue that *Harry Potter* fans are subordinate to and dominated by corporations, but they are resistant, too. For Fiske, popular culture involves meaning making in the form of excorporation – taking objects from mass culture and infusing them with their own meaning. Fiske's famous example is blue jeans – produced by the "dominant" group and made unique by the "subordinate" who tears them, fades them, dyes them – at which point the manufacturers reincorporate fans' modifications and produce torn, bleached jeans for sale, thereby completing the cycle. *Harry Potter* fan culture exemplifies how fans excorporate Rowling's storyline across multiple transmedia platforms, creating their own art, literature, festivals, and, with the Harry Potter Alliance, even activism, demonstrating how fans mimic Rowling's own charitable work and/or interpret the books' values (such as the triumph of good over evil) for their own political messages. Pottermore, too, was inspired by fan content. Warner Bros. has

---

[42] J. Fiske, *Reading the Popular*, 2nd edn. (Oxford and New York: Routledge, 2011), 1.

[43] J. Fiske, *Understanding Popular Culture* (Oxford and New York: Routledge, 2010), 67.

focused on attempting to control fans' content and message – creating "model" fans, whose labor continues to promote the franchise.

Collins describes the impact of the digital realm, in which Amazon's virtual reading communities (to which one might add Goodreads and others) make it

> abundantly clear that the need to demonstrate one's personal taste in terms of the books one chooses forms an essential part of the pleasures of reading. That books can now function just as effectively as "mere" consumer items such as clothing or furniture as a public manifestation of one's taste – and that this is a conviction held by "mass audiences" and not just intellectuals of the traditional variety – is a major factor in transforming literary culture into popular culture.[44]

According to Matt Hills,

> the shifting terrain of a "digital habitus," articulated with multiple intertextualities and participatory cultures, suggests that fan studies should no longer be drawing on a restricted view of "highbrow" cultural capital as resolutely opposed to fan cultural capital (and hence as irrelevant to the study of fandom). Instead, fan practices of "emerging" and generational cultural capital are becoming ever more apparent in relation to the digital afterlives of Austen and Shakespeare.[45]

Fandom and Ownership

In his 2012 text *Textual Poachers*, Jenkins delineates a set of rules that constitute fandom, which are summarized below. Jenkins sees "fandom" as

[44] Collins, *Bring on the Books*, 78.

[45] M. Hills, "Implicit fandom in the fields of theatre, art, and literature: Studying 'fans' beyond fan discourses." In P. Booth (ed.), *A Companion to Media Fandom and Fan Studies* (New York: John Wiley & Sons), 488.

"the unofficial fan community" participating in a cultural commodity: "Fandom recognizes no clear-cut line between artists and consumers; all fans are potential writers whose talents need to be discovered, nurtured, and promoted and who may be able to make a contribution, however modest, to the cultural wealth of the larger community."[46]

Not only is the creation of products shared between artists and consumers, but ownership of such cultural products is also shared. While Jenkins is writing about television, the same is true for the *Harry Potter* transmedia universe. Jenkins writes: "Once television characters enter into a broader circulation, intrude into our living rooms, pervade the fabric of our society, they belong to their audience and not simply to the artists who originated them."[47] And indeed, this idea reflects Barthes's, in his "Death of the Author" essay: "writing is the destruction of every voice, of every point of origin. Writing is that neutral, composite, oblique space where our subject slips away, the negative where all identity is lost, starting with the very identity of the body writing."[48]

For corporate owners, this perception of collective ownership in fan fiction and festivals – the notion that characters belong to artists and consumers – is problematic, as it potentially impacts profits. Festival organizers, who might have a general understanding of copyright law and trademark law, may not understand how community-created festivals are problematic in the eyes of Warner Bros. although increased intervention from Warner during 2017 and 2018 in shutting down festivals is becoming publicized. For Jenkins, fandom has an important social aspect; fans "translate the reception process into social interaction with other fans."[49] It is not surprising that fans were so upset when Pottermore disabled in-site commenting and essentially removed social aspects of the site at its 2015 relaunch.

Fans for a Day versus Fans Every Day

While scholars have attempted to distinguish between types of fans (for example, Abercrombie and Longhurst suggested "fans, cultists and

[46] Jenkins, *Textual Poachers*, 280. [47] Ibid.

[48] R. Barthes, *Image, Music, Text*, translated by S. Heath (New York: Hill and Wang, 1977), 142.

[49] Jenkins, *Textual Poachers*, 278.

enthusiasts"[50]), *Harry Potter* presents a unique example when it comes to distinguishing a general audience from hard-core fans. I would argue that with *Harry Potter*, there is fluidity and overlap, for example at festivals, where hard-core fans meet the general readership. It is not necessarily visible to the eye to which group anyone belongs, as many are in costume, and all are participating. The difference might be those who are fans for a day, versus those who are fans every day. General audience members, or fans for a day, who might not otherwise write fan fiction or participate, still enjoy dressing up, drinking Butterbeer, playing wizardly games, and bringing their families. More zealous fans, who participate in fan fiction and more, might also bring their families to festivals, or serve as organizers. In the Harry Potter Alliance (HPA), activists are intergenerational too, as younger fans might participate in high school or college branches of the HPA, but grandmothers, mothers, and daughters might attend the Granger Leadership Academy together.

Andy Ruddock offers a useful way to distinguish between fans: "The question is how far are fans analogous to general audiences. Those who have written about fans differ as to how far this is their goal, but Fiske (1992) bases much of his thinking on the resistive opportunities offered by mass culture on the idea that fans differ from everyday audiences in degree rather than kind."[51]

This concept of "degrees" of fandom is also connected to passion and emotion, both of which are are important components of fandom and drive the affective relationship with cultural products. According to Ruddock,

> Passion and an uncontrolled emotional attachment are associated with an uncritical intellectual weakness. Since fans of popular culture often allow their favourite shows or performers to take over their lives, they are thus representative of the worst aspects of mass culture: its ability to produce political complacency by allowing people to withdraw into

---

[50] Quoted in M. Hills, "Fiske's 'textual productivity' and digital fandom: Web 2.0 democratization versus fan distinction?" *Participations*, 10 (2013), 134.

[51] A. Ruddock, *Understanding Audiences* (London: SAGE, 2001), 156.

a fantasy world of imaginary friends. Fans, according to this
critique, replace the social with the parasocial, wherein their
social network consists of mediated personalities with whom
they can have no real contact.[52]

Hills describes cases of "high cultural fandom" as that which occurs around
opera, theater, and even certain musicals, such as *Hamilton*, where lines
between high and pop culture blur.[53] Applying Bourdieu's field theory to
the *Harry Potter* phenomenon, it appears that elements of the pop cultural
fandom have higher aspirations.[54] Hills categorizes Bourdieu's fields
as "bounded spaces with their own distinct forms of recognition."[55]
Whether we are talking about fans writing and critically evaluating each
other's fan fictions, or festivals that incorporate high cultural elements, such
as Odense's Harry Potter Festival, elements of the *Harry Potter* universe
approach high cultural spaces not typically associated with pop culture. In
examining *Harry Potter*, Bourdieu's poles of autonomous versus heteronomous are not sufficient. Hills has complicated and reinterpreted Bourdieu's
modes of production, allowing for a more nuanced quadrant depiction
rather than a binary model,[56] discussed in the next section. Indeed, *Harry
Potter*'s transmedia products and the participation within them align better
with this model. In fact, in evaluating *Harry Potter* in terms of Bourdieu's
field theory, *Harry Potter* merits a field of its own.

The Harry Potter Field

The field of cultural production, as applied to *Harry Potter*, has a very clear,
top-down power structure, but even though Warner Bros. is dominant with
ultimate power to control certain fan activity via cease-and-desist letters and
lawsuits, the relationship between dominant (corporate) and subordinate
(fans) is a codependent one (see Figure 1).

   According to Bourdieu,

---

[52] Ruddock, *Understanding Audiences*, 154.   [53] Hills, "Implicit fandom," 477.

[54] P. Bourdieu, *The Field of Cultural Production: Essays on Art and Literature*
(New York: Cambridge University Press, 1993).

[55] Hills, "Implicit fandom," 479.   [56] Ibid., 480.

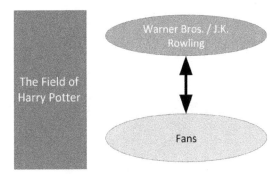

Figure 1 The field according to Harry

> the literary or artistic field is at all times the site of a struggle
> between the two principles of hierarchization: the hetero-
> nomous principle, favourable to those who dominate the
> field economically and politically (e.g. "bourgeois art") and
> the autonomous principle (e.g. "art for art's sake"), which
> those of its advocates who are least endowed with specific
> capital tend to identify with degree of independence from
> the economy, seeing temporal failure as a sign of election
> and success as a sign of compromise.[57]

In applying Bourdieu's field theory to *Harry Potter*, and expanding it to
incorporate Hills's quadrants, there are four areas (see Figure 2).

Autonomous-autonomous productions represent the purest form of
artistic endeavor and the highest in symbolic value, "marked by their
'purity' and 'authenticity' within the field."[58]

The autonomous-heteronomous quadrant "corresponds to cultural products intended for a specialist audience."[59] Because *Harry Potter* occupies
a transmedia universe of overlapping and codependent products, a nested
version of Hills's quadrant is preferable, as seen in Figure 2.

[57] Bourdieu, *Field of Cultural Production*, 40 (emphasis is my own).
[58] Hills, "Implicit fandom", 480. [59] Ibid.

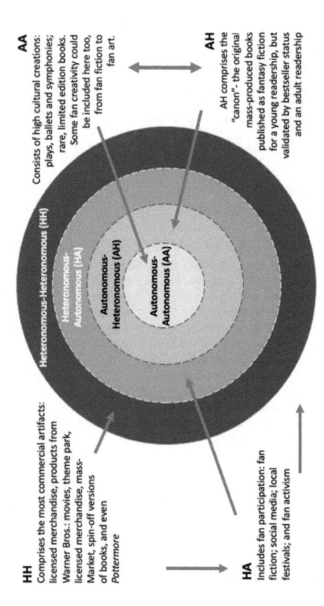

AA

Consists of high cultural creations: plays, ballets and symphonies; rare, limited edition books. Some fan creativity could be included here too, from fan fiction to fan art.

AH

AH comprises the "canon"– the original mass-produced books published as fantasy fiction for a young readership, but validated by bestseller status and an adult readership

HH

Comprises the most commercial artifacts: licensed merchandise, products from Warner Bros.: movies, theme park, licensed merchandise, mass-Market, spin-off versions of books, and even *Pottermore*

HA

Includes fan participation: fan fiction; social media; local festivals; and fan activism

Figure 2 Bourdieu's nested and expanded "poles," inspired by Hills's (2018) quadrant model, and reinterpreted through the lens of *Harry Potter*

The heteronomous-heteronomous sphere "represents commercial culture consumed precisely as commercial culture . . . heteronomous fans will happily act as consumers of merchandise; attend highly corporate convention events [such as Comic-Con]; pay inflated sums for autographs and 'photo opportunities' with celebrities."[60]

The heteronomous-autonomous quadrant "represents a mode of cultural production intended to be highly commercial but which is embraced and consumed by a neo-cognoscenti that takes on its own cultural differentiation. The social emergence of fandom achieves this level in relation to pop-cultural forms, meaning that texts such as *Star Trek* and *Star Wars* are culturally elevated as a result of the enduring fan knowledge they sustain and the 'classic' status they take on."[61]

In terms of *Harry Potter* fandom, the lines between autonomous-autonomous and heteronomous-heteronomous are blurred. Because it is a book first, and reading is a literary activity associated with high culture,[62] *Harry Potter* technically belongs in the realm of high culture. But as a series written and published primarily for a young audience – despite the fact that as a crossover series it has an adult readership – it is relegated to the low cultural status of children's literature. Beverly Lyon Clarke argues that the *New York Times*'s children's best-seller list was created not in praise of children's literature, but rather to ghettoize it and to keep *Harry Potter* titles off of the adult list.[63] Additionally, in the years since its publication *Harry Potter* has appeared in various commercial formats, including movies, toys, and theme parks, which anchors it firmly in "popular literary culture."[64] So while *Harry Potter* may stretch toward high cultural arenas, it exists firmly in the realm of pop culture.

In terms of economic capital, while in the years since *Harry Potter*'s publication YA novels such as the *Twilight* saga by Stephenie Meyer, the

[60] Ibid., 481. [61] Ibid.

[62] P. Bourdieu, *Distinction: A Social Critique of the Judgement of Taste* (Cambridge, MA: Harvard University Press, 1984).

[63] B. L. Clark, *Kiddie Lit: The Cultural Construction of Children's Literature in America* (Baltimore, MD: John Hopkins University Press, 2004).

[64] Collins, *Bring on the Books*, 3.

Hunger Games trilogy by Suzanne Collins, *The Hate U Give* by Angie Johnson and more have gone to auction and earned six-figure advances, the reality is that first-time YA author advances are significantly smaller. Even here, *Harry Potter* was an outlier: a book by an unknown author that earned a significant advance in its US auction and subsequently landed on the *New York Times* best-seller list – both of which were highly unusual phenomena for a book published by a press such as Scholastic, which specializes in works for children and young adults. Since then, it has earned the author unprecedented economic capital. As such, *Harry Potter* exists in a field of its own, as a pop culture children's product with adult appeal.

With certain spin-off products, J. K. Rowling's authorial role bends toward the autonomous pole, as she stretches into "screen writing" (the movies) and "dramaturgy" (the *Cursed Child* play). It is unlikely that anyone would contest that J. K. Rowling is the author of the *Harry Potter* series. But authorship does begin to blur with adaptation, as a book becomes a movie, a theme park, and licensed merchandise. As Amanda Stephenson argues, while J. K. Rowling never received any screenwriting credit in the *Harry Potter* films, publicity material emphasizes her authorial role as creator of the books, despite the fact that Chris Columbus (director) and Steve Cloves (screenwriter) had significant roles in the adaptations.[65] Authorship in the *Harry Potter* series is completely associated with J. K. Rowling, and not with Warner Bros., and this is in part because of the prestige, the branding, and the subsequent marketability that J. K. Rowling lends to the project.

Several scholars have written about authors' branded identities.[66] In fact, Agathe Nicolas describes Rowling's intentionally blurred authorial identity

---

[65] A. Stephenson, *The Constructions of Authorship and Audience in the Production and Consumption of Children's Film Adaptations*, unpublished PhD dissertation, University of Southampton, 2016.

[66] A. Nicolas, "Formes de représentation, impératif d'actualité et enjeux de pouvoir sur les dispositifs numériques : L'Exemple de J. K. Rowling et du site," *Mémoires du livre*, 9 (2018), 1–39; M. E. Thérenty and A. Wrona, "L'Écrivain comme marque: Agenda" [The author as a brand: Agenda], retrieved from www .fabula.org/actualites/l-ecrivain-comme-marque_57463.php;

within the larger *Harry Potter* franchise. "Dans le cas de J. K. Rowling, nous avons pu constater la complexification de la figure d'auteur par son 'devenir fiction,' sa transformation en une entité d'ordre quasi fictionnel."[67] ["In the case of J. K. Rowling, we see the author-figure complicated by becoming fictional – her transformation into a quasi-fictional being" (my own translation).] Nicolas also describes how the partnership with Warner Bros. has transformed Rowling into a branded author. As far as *Harry Potter* is concerned, Rowling is both creator (as concerning copyright) and owner (or co-owner with Warner Bros. as concerning trademark) of the *Harry Potter* brand.

> L'invisibilisation du collectif au profit de la valorisation de la figure d'auteur tend à montrer que, malgré les évolutions de la notion de l'autorité d'auteur liées aux caractéristiques culturelles et techniques des dispositifs numériques, la stratégie communicationnelle de ce site internet, lieu de mise en scène de l'auteur, de ses œuvres et de leur circulation transmédiatique, est construite sur l'image d'une figure d'auteur puissante et inaccessible.[68] [Making collective creative contributions invisible in favor of valorizing the author shows that despite the evolutions of the notion of authorial authority, as related to the cultural and technical characteristics of digital devices, the communication strategy of this website [Pottermore], on which the author, her works, and their transmedia circulation is staged, is built upon the image of a powerful and inaccessible author (my own translation).]

Moran writes that literary celebrity reformulates

> authorship within the literary marketplace and [uses] it as the repository of all kinds of conflicting cultural meanings

---

[67] M. E. Thérenty and A. Wrona, eds., *L'Écrivain comme marque* [The author as a brand] (Paris: Presses universitaires de la Sorbonne, 2018), 11.

[68] Nicolas, "Formes de représentation," 19.

and values. The same might be said, in fact, for celebrity culture in general, which reifies individuals and allows them to be used by capitalist society in a variety of ways – as market stimuli, as representations of ideal social types, as focal points for the desires and longings of audiences and so on.[69]

Even though others are closely involved in the production of each new extension, the audience expects the Rowling brand to be attached to each one. For the corporate owners it is important that she is perceived as having a strong creative role. As a star author with celebrity status, Rowling's name attached to everything *Harry Potter* provides authenticity and serves as a key marketing tool. Adding to her status as an "ideal social type," Rowling was presented by Queen Elizabeth with the Order of the Companion of Honour for her charitable works (including her foundation, Lumos), elevating her social capital – and her prestige. "[Barthes] aims to show that the privileged figure of the author is a modern invention, the product of bourgeois society's discovery of 'the prestige of the individual.'"[70]

In addition to her increased cultural, social, and economic capital, Rowling also accrues significant political capital via her tweets. As of November 18, 2018, she had 14,500,000 followers on Twitter, where she is an outspoken critic of US president Donald Trump and of the UK's Brexit deal, and often responds to fans to argue for a stance she has taken, whether she is defending the casting of Johnny Depp in a *Fantastic Beasts* movie after he was accused of domestic violence, or asserting her right to revise her books post-publication. As John Fiske wrote, the cultural is always political,[71] and nowhere is this more the case than with J. K. Rowling.

Fan Community and the Public Sphere

In his work *The Structural Transformation of the Public Sphere*, the German philosopher Jürgen Habermas describes the "public sphere" as sites where

[69] J. Moran, *Star Authors: Literary Celebrity in America* (Sterling, VA: Pluto Press, 2000), 60.

[70] Moran, *Star Authors*, 59. [71] Fiske, *Reading the Popular*.

individuals exchange ideas and engage in active and inclusive critical dialogue.[72] From the transformation of small discussion societies in eighteenth-century salons to the twentieth century's mass publics created via journalism and media, Habermas argues that mass media has a negative effect on the public sphere, and moves us from a sphere dominated by intellectual opinion and debate to one dominated by propaganda. His criticism of the twentieth-century public sphere is grounded in the transformation of the field of journalism from one formerly based on "conviction" to one based on "commerce."[73] Weber[74] introduces the idea of including the affective and social roles that publics have in the twenty-first century, and this concept helps explain participation in popular cultural forums, to which access is limited only by language and access to the Internet.

While *Harry Potter* fans may not be creating a new cosmopolitan political order, they are politically empowered, whether they are organizing a social media revolt to shape the content of a corporate-owned fan site, organizing festivals despite corporate efforts to restrain them, or engaging in social change through activism and volunteering via the Harry Potter Alliance.

On his "Confessions of an Aca-Fan" blog, Henry Jenkins wrote: "as critics such as Suzanne Scott and Julie Levine Russo have noted, transmedia practices tend to priviledge [sic] some kinds of fans over others, constructing model fans and thus seeking to set the terms of how fans relate to the material."[75] Yet while creators of transmedia products, such as Rowling and – by extension – Warner Bros., may have the goal of creating model fans who will help them via their immaterial and affective labor to shape fandom in particular ways, not all fans want to participate in prescribed

[72] J. Habermas, *The Structural Transformation of the Public Sphere* (Cambridge, MA: MIT Press, 1989 [1962]).

[73] Ibid.

[74] M. Weber, *Literary Festivals and Contemporary Book Culture* (London: Palgrave Macmillan, 2018).

[75] H. Jenkins, "Three reasons why Pottermore matters," *Confessions of an Aca Fan*, June 24, 2011, http://henryjenkins.org/blog/2011/06/three_reasons_why_pottermore_m.html

activities – or to participate in the way that corporate owners would prefer. This Element explores three ways in which politicized fans circumnavigate corporate owners in order to experience their fandom on their own terms. Corporate owners walk a fine line between wanting to protect their copyrighted and trademarked content and wanting to maintain good relations with the fans. Even if Rowling and Warner are not pleased with the HPA, which they may not be, in part because of the organization's involvement in changing the manufacturer of their chocolate licensing deal, it would be terrible publicity if Rowling or Warner wanted to shut down a non-profit organization whose mission is, "We're changing the world by making activism accessible through the power of story. Since 2005, we've engaged millions of fans through our work for equality, human rights, and literacy."[76]

In the context of Harry Potter's online fandom, the digital realm contributes to a structural transformation or, rather, an extension of Habermas's public sphere into a digital public sphere, in which corporations are free to take as much from fans as the fans get from their participation – in terms of their shared ideas, information, taste, and labor.

Others have described versions of digital public spheres, such as Bruns and Highfield, who depict Twitter as a "personal" public sphere, in that users can use "@mention" to discuss a topic with a particular "@user," limiting a conversation to those who follow each user.[77] Rowling does this frequently with her mentions of @realDonaldTrump or @fans, and when she engages in dialogue with her fans, either by liking tweets, retweeting, or the ultimate – responding directly – fans are beyond excited, as shown below:

> Should i change my twitter profile to "J K. Rowling liked my tweet". Am i basically famous now?????[78]

[76] Harry Potter Alliance, "What we do," 2015, www.thehpalliance.org/what_we_do

[77] A. Bruns and T. Highfield, "Is Habermas on Twitter?" In C. Christensen, G. Enli, A. Bruns, E. Sokgerbo, and A. O. Larsson (eds.), *Social Media and the Public Sphere* (New York and Oxford: Routledge, 2015).

[78] A. Pollock [@alainapol22], (2018, April 24). "Should i change my twitter profile to 'J K. Rowling liked my tweet'. Am i basically famous now?????" Twitter,

For Habermas, the public sphere is infused with politics, and there are many political implications of a digital public sphere that extends from fan communities to the corporations with whom fans interact, from proprietary platforms to Twitter.

Rowling, too, engages in Twitter activism, and her tweets receive many accolades, such as the example seen above, but also much criticism, whether she is using Twitter to criticize the US president or to revise the *Harry Potter* canon. In 2007 she made the canon-shattering announcement that the Hogwarts headmaster Albus Dumbledore was gay,[79] and the discussions of sexual orientation in relation to the series continue years later. In 2014, in response to a tweet from a fan asking if there are LGBT students in modern-day Hogwarts, Rowling responded with an illustration and a statement about not living in closets, referencing Harry Potter's childhood bedroom, which was in a cupboard under the stairs. Dumbledore's sexuality as omitted from the series has an historical precedent as well, as gay characters were absent in the original *Star Trek* series.[80] Ruddock describes Jenkins's research that demonstrated how, for some fans, the show's sexual ambiguity was its attraction, but that a growing frustration with the lack of gay characters led to the development of organized fan groups who appealed to the producer for change. "Thus fan groups and fan research are part of a project that seeks not just to understand and interpret media texts, but to alter the course of their production."[81]

April 24, 2018, https://twitter.com/search?q=Should%20i%20change%20my%20twitter%20profile%20to%20%E2%80%9CJ%20K.%20Rowling%20liked%20my%20tweet%E2%80%9D.%20Am%20i%20basically%20famous%20now&src=typd

[79] EdwardTLC, "J. K. Rowling at Carnegie Hall reveals Dumbledore is gay," The Leaky Cauldron, October 20, 2007, www.the-leaky-cauldron.org/2007/10/20/j-k-rowling-at-carnegie-hall-reveals-dumbledore-is-gay-neville-marries-hannah-abbott-and-scores-more

[80] H. Jenkins, "*Star Trek* rerun, reread, rewritten: Fan writing as textual poaching," *Critical Studies in Mass Communication*, 5 (1988), 85–107; A. Ruddock, *Investigating Audiences* (London: SAGE, 2007).

[81] Ruddock, *Investigating Audiences*, 80.

In a January 2018 interview in *Vanity Fair*, director David Yates said that the film *Fantastic Beasts 2* would not explicitly signal Dumbledore's sexuality,[82] which reignited the conversation on social media. In response to the article, disappointed fans tweeted to @Rowling, and Rowling, seemingly frustrated, tweeted back on January 31, 2018 that the film was based on one out of five screenplays that she had written, which no one had read (because they had not been published). But fans were not silenced. Mostly, fans viewed J. K. Rowling as being inauthentic in her support of gay rights because she had waited many years to declare that Dumbledore was gay, wondering about her motive for suddenly making him so.[83] For example, Twitter user O Hayes [@ohaaayes] tweeted:

> How on earth you [Rowling] carry on pretending to be a progressive icon is beyond me. Retroactively deciding that "there was a Jewish guy at Hogwarts" is not representation. Neither was deciding Dumbledore was gay but conveniently leaving it out of the text.[84]

The question of representation of marginalized groups (or lack thereof) is just one of many political issues that come up in the digital sphere of *Harry Potter* fandom. *Harry Potter* fans experience deeply personal connections with the series, as discussed next.

---

[82] L. Bradley, "Fantastic beasts: The crimes of Grindelwald and Dumbledore's vexing sexuality," *Vanity Fair*, February 15, 2018, www.vanityfair.com/hollywood/2018/11/fantastic-beasts-the-crimes-of-grindelwald-dumbledore-gay-queerbaiting

[83] For examples of more tweets from fans and J. K. Rowling's responses, see L. Respers, "J. K. Rowling responds to gay Dumbledore controversy," February 1, 2018, *CNN Entertainment*, www.cnn.com/2018/02/01/entertainment/jk-rowling-dumbledore-gay/index.html

[84] O Hayes [@ohaaayes], "How on earth ... ", April 21, 2018, *Twitter* https://twitter.com/search?f=tweets&q=there%20was%20a%20Jewish%20guy%20at%20Hogwarts%E2%80%9D%20is%20not%20representation.%20Neither%20was%20deciding%20Dumbledore%20was%20gay%20&src=typd

Sentiments

Young adults report that having a connection to *Harry Potter* has helped them get through major life issues, from divorce, to stress, to loss, to identity development. Librarian and fan fiction writer K. W. described how *Harry Potter* helped her deal with personal trauma:

> It's my comfort, honestly, and I don't know if this is too much information, but reading *Harry Potter* got me through my divorce recently. Like if I didn't have that to read at night to really just shut my brain off and focus on something else, I don't know what I would have done ... like, to stabilize myself.[85]

Another reader, a 25-year-old male doctoral student in the UK, described *Harry Potter* as providing him with stress relief. He said that re-reading the books in the evening helps him relax. For O. P., a 38-year-old librarian and mother of a 14-year-old daughter and an 18-year-old son, *Harry Potter* became a source of comfort after she lost her mother. O. P. had initially become a huge fan as a 24-year-old adult, when she watched the film version of *Harry Potter and the Chamber of Secrets* with her mother shortly before her mother passed away. For O. P., *Harry Potter* represents an emotional connection with her mother and is a way of keeping the memory of her alive. While her children are also fans of the series, she says she is the bigger fan, paying about US$30 a month to subscribe to J. K. Rowling's Wizarding World-themed "Loot Crate"[86] to obtain a box of assorted fan merchandise every month. *Harry Potter* fandom also translates into her work as a children's librarian, as she runs an annual celebration of Harry's birthday at the library where she works. She provides themed games, treats, a wand-choosing station at which kids are blindfolded and "selected" by wands she makes herself ahead of time, and a green screen where participants can take

[85] K. W., interview, 2017.

[86] Loot Crate, "J. K. Rowling's wizarding world," 2018, www.lootcrate.com /crates/wizarding-world

photos with different characters and backgrounds from the books and movies, such as Platform 9¾ and Hogwarts Castle.[87]

For others, fan communities provide a sense of family. For one fan, C. M., her *Harry Potter* fandom represents love and community. She calls the Harry Potter Alliance her "found family." C. M. grew up in a small town in the midwestern United States, where she felt marginalized as a member of the LGBTQIA+ community, and she says that *Harry Potter* opened her mind to feminism (via fandom), and to LGBTQIA+ rights, which comprise a significant part of the Harry Potter Alliance.[88] It is not surprising that C. M. discovered both feminism and LGBTQIA+ community members in fandom and in the Harry Potter Alliance – rather than within the books, where both are lacking. Scholars such as Tison Pugh and David Wallace have criticized the books as emphasizing heteronormativity, and while women do hold positions of power – Hermione is "one of the most important characters,"[89] and Minerva McGonagall serves as Deputy Headmistress of Hogwarts[90] – those positions tend to be second-in-command spots, and ultimately, the series is a "boy's story"[91]:

> The *Harry Potter* series has not (at least in the first six books) shown us an emerging hero who learns anything about the operation of sexism and heterosexism in his world. Indeed, the effects of heteronormative heroism in the *Harry Potter* books are numerous and disturbing: non-normative sexual identities are completely absent, possible queer-affirming readings are problematized, women and girls are presented in subservient and sexualized roles, and Harry's own character is forced into a narrow action-hero role that requires the death or removal of any competitors.[92]

[87] O. P., interview, 2017. [88] C. M., interview, 2017.

[89] T. Pugh and D. L. Wallace, "Heteronormative heroism and queering the school story in JK Rowling's Harry Potter series," *Children's Literature Association Quarterly*, 31 (2006), 268.

[90] Ibid. [91] Pugh and Wallace, "Heteronormative heroism," 267.

[92] Push and Wallace, "Heteronormative heroism," 275.

It is not surprising that fans and scholars were offended at J. K. Rowling's outing of Dumbledore. As Pugh and Wallace write in a 2008 postscript to their 2006 article: "If Dumbledore's homosexuality was not important enough to include within the narrative trajectories of seven novels, mentioning it after the series ends comes a bit too little, too late."[93]

Why do Fans Participate?

As scholars such as Plante et al. have found, "fan groups, far from being an individualistic mindless consumption of media, can have a potentially deep and meaningful impact on [fans'] values, identity, and potentially [their] behavior."[94] What causes fans to engage with *Harry Potter* is their affective relationship with the brand, and the sense of community it inspires. One of the most important things that unites fans around *Potter* fandom, however they choose to define that for themselves, or however they participate, is their love[95] for the series, and their willingness to contribute their labor for the series. Fans' immaterial and affective labor[96] has proven far more effective than any marketing the publishers could have paid for.

Harry Potter branding works two ways. First, the brand's corporate agents – Bloomsbury in the United Kingdom, Scholastic in the United States, Sony, and Warner Bros. – as well as the author herself, established the brand. Fans' love for the brand led to their engagement, but fans and corporate owners are hardly equals. Corporate owners have shut down proprietary sites, as they did with the first rendition of the Pottermore site, when fans' participation became unwieldy, difficult to monitor, or overly critical. Fans' labor can be exploited on sites such as Goodreads (owned by Amazon.com) and Epic Reads (owned by HarperCollins), where fans' comments and feedback can be used to shape the content of future books

---

[93] T. Pugh and D. L. Wallace, "A postscript to 'Heteronormative heroism and queering the school story in JK Rowling's Harry Potter series,'" *Children's Literature Association Quarterly*, 33 (2008), 191.

[94] Plante et al., "'One of us'," 61.

[95] M. Coté and J. Pybus, "Learning to immaterial labor 2.0: Myspace and Social Networks," *Ephemera*, 7 (2007), 88–106.

[96] Terranova, "Free labor."

in a series. Fans' true criticism is pushed to the fringes of social media, especially Twitter, where users can generate hashtag conversations and build consensus and community, without oversight. Second, fans become branded too, via their participation. Their affective relationship with the series drives fans to join in with fandom, whether it is participating in fan fiction, organizing and attending festivals, or, after growing up with the fandom, engaging in more adult activities via the books, such as the Harry Potter Alliance. This relationship, in turn, supports the fandom and subsequently sales of books, movies, and related products. For *Harry Potter* fans, affect for the series is deeply connected to their own emotional ownership:

> A further aspect of media studies of audiences and one particularly pertinent to the literary festival is the distinction between fan groups and the broader media audience. Ross and Nightingale define fans as "specialized audiences with very intensified relationships to content" ... emphasizing their active and organized production of supplementary content, and their sense of emotional ownership of the text deriving from this dedication.[97]

As we will see later herein, for fans, *Harry Potter* inspires deep connections and feelings of comfort, nostalgia, and identity.

Identity, Community, and the Harry Potter Generation

The term "*Harry Potter* Generation" is used freely across mass media,[98] fan sites (Mugglenet), and even in scholarly literature,[99] but rarely is it clearly

---

[97] M. Weber, "Conceptualizing audience experience at the literary festival," *Continuum: Journal of Media & Cultural Studies*, 29 (2014), 88.

[98] L. Prendergast, "Harry Potter and the Millennial mind: How J. K. Rowling shaped the political thinking of a generation," June 2017, *The Spectator*, www.spectator.co.uk /2017/06/harry-potter-and-the-millenial-mind/; D. Wyatt, "Why Harry Potter's aged 35, not 26," *The Independent*, July 31, 2015, www.independent.co.uk/arts-entertainment/books/news/why-harry-potters-aged-35-not-26-10430209.html

[99] C. K. Farr, *A Wizard of Their Age: Critical Essays from the Harry Potter Generation* (Albany, NY: State University of New York Press, 2015).

defined. Alyssa Jeanette, writing on Mugglenet, states: "When it comes to *Harry Potter*, there's a similar parallel: if you weren't Harry's age, you're not a part of his capital-g-Generation."[100] She further states that Harry Potter's birthday is generally accepted as July 31, 1980.[101] However, there is a slight twist in calculating his age, because in the first book, published in 1997, Harry was eleven years old, which technically would make his birth year 1986. Mugglenet accepts the *Harry Potter* Generation as those born between 1980 and 1986.

Prendergast argues that anyone under 35 automatically knows basics about the series, such as a description of the four houses of Hogwarts. She writes that "The 'Potterverse' is the millennial universe."[102] According to the Pew Research Center, millennials are those born roughly between 1981 and 1996.[103] For the purposes of this text, those in the *Harry Potter* Generation are those born between 1980 and 1996, who grew up reading the new books in the series each year as they were published.

Fans' affective and emotional connections with the texts is what encourages them to participate in almost anything connected to the series. Fans are able to identify with specific characters from the book, such as one fan fiction writer who related to Hermione:

> And you find aspects of yourselves in the characters like, when I read it I was like, oh my god, Hermione is a bookworm, too and she gets shit done and people respect

[100] A. Jennette, "Defining the 'Harry Potter' generation," Mugglenet, September 29, 2013, www.mugglenet.com/2013/09/defining-the-harry-potter-generation/

[101] Calculations on Harry's age stem from a 500-year celebration of Nearly Headless Nick in the second book, in which he is described to have died in 1492. Five hundred years later means that the second book was set in 1992, when Harry was twelve years old.

[102] L. Prendergast, "Harry Potter and the millennial mind," *The Spectator*, June 2017, www.spectator.co.uk/2017/06/harry-potter-and-the-millenial-mind/

[103] Pew Research Center, "Defining generations: Where millennials end and post millennials begin," March 1, 2018, www.pewresearch.org/facttank/2018/03/01/defining-generations-where-millennials-end-and-post-millennials-begin/

> her and yeah, she gets made fun of but as the series goes on
> you know I think Ron even says, or Harry in the seventh
> book, "if it weren't for Hermione we'd be dead."[104]

Others identify more generally with the books on a larger scale, feeling that there is room for all at Hogwarts, including those who are marginalized:

> And I feel like that is why you see so many, why [*Harry
> Potter*] fandom is a big space for women, it kind of always
> has been. And then, more recently, you're also seeing other
> marginalized groups – and people of color, people of dif-
> ferent sexualities – being like, you know, I'm going to
> change this character, this world around to suit my liking.[105]

In addition to the fan empowerment that is enabled by their participation, the sense of community that exists among *Harry Potter* fans is enormously instrumental in ensuring ongoing participation. Ranjana Das writes of the sense of belonging "to a group of others, with whom [one] feels solidarity and bonding, to an entire generation."[106] Fans are connected by their love for the series and its characters, but also via their labor for the series, as they continue to promote the series by writing about it (on fan sites), by engaging in cosplay (at festivals), and by volunteering and promoting *Harry Potter* culture as one that is interested in acting for the greater good, which connects to the morals and values embedded in the series.

Ommundsen writes in 2004: "The increasing commodification of books and authors is frequently evoked as signs of the 'dumbing down' of serious art, its contamination by popular culture, its 'selling out' of high-minded pursuits for the sake of entertainment and material gain."[107]

---

[104] K. W., interview, 2017. [105] C. M., interview, 2017.

[106] R. Das, "'I've walked this street': Readings of 'reality' in British young people's reception of Harry Potter," *Journal of Children and Media*, 10 (2016), 348.

[107] W. Ommundsen, "Sex, soap and sainthood: Beginning to theorise literary celebrity," *Journal of the Association for the Study of Australian Literature*, 3 (2004), 52.

Yet the *Harry Potter* series never claimed to be high art. Not only was it published for young people but also the books were planned and published as a series, placing them in a particular mass market niche in terms of publishing, which is excluded from the realms of high art, compared to an original work of fiction first published in hardcover for an adult audience. As a contemporary series with a living author (as opposed to "classic" works which exist beyond the life of the author), *Harry Potter* is always firmly embedded in the realm of popular culture – especially because of its status as a transmedia blockbuster appearing across media channels. Writers for young people have certain freedoms that writers of literature for adults do not. While children's literature has its own mechanisms (awards, reviews, notable lists) for determining distinction, sales are certainly not dependent on these mechanisms, as young readers have a distinct voice in determining whether or not a particular book or series will be successful. For example, the *Twilight* series received weak reviews in traditional (i.e., adult-based) review sites, and was ignored by awards committees, but when teens were involved in expressing their opinions on the American Library Association's Best Books for Young Adults committee, the books were chosen as top contenders for years.[108]

Who Owns Harry, Anyway? Resisting the Updates

This idea of *Harry Potter* prestige translates also into the fan fiction community, as fan fiction writers have felt deeply connected to – and protective of – the original books, both by carefully and collectively analyzing the stories as they were written and now by reacting to and resisting Rowling's revisions of the canon, which, as well as statements about Dumbledore's sexuality, include claims that Hermione is black. Fan fiction writers have their own sense of ownership over the characters in the books as well, and these revisions often upset them. As a fan fiction writer told me, fan fiction writers at times disregard Rowling's updates. K. W. described one author who added a note to his or her fic: "I'm ignoring everything J. K. Rowling is saying, I'm just going on what's in the books."[109] At times, fan fiction

---

[108] Martens, *Publishers*. [109] K. W., interview, 2017.

writers favor just using the *Potter* universe as it appears in the books; at other times they might violate the statements of later books but stay with the "canon" for the earlier books. K. W. recalled, "on livejournal back in the day, I was very involved in talking with other [fan fiction] authors and discussing really in-depth analysis of what we thought this chapter [of the book] meant or what outcomes that the whole might have or what, you know, characters were going to end up together and things like that"[110]

Now that the books are complete, K. W. says, fans are more likely to discuss aspects of Pottermore they don't like, and the new information that might change their understanding of the books. Fan fiction writer K. E. describes Rowling's revisions as "the author's head-canon,"[111] and considers them to be irrelevant. While it is not clear what motivates Rowling to make these revisions, after the audience broke out in cheers when she announced Dumbledore's sexuality in 2007, she reportedly said: "I would have told you earlier if I knew it would make you so happy."[112]

From Canon to Fanon

In fact, *Harry Potter* "fanon" vs. "canon" discussions have become so nuanced that scholar Lauren Camacci actually breaks "canon" down into five different levels. The first, "canon," refers to the original works, or to the original *Harry Potter* books. "Alt canon" refers to the movies. "Para-canon," which plays on Gennette's concept of paratext, refers to all *Harry Potter*-related artifacts. The "fanon" is all fan-related content, and then "meta-canon" refers to J. K. Rowling's updates and edits via companion novels, Twitter, screenplays, and Pottermore content.[113]

---

[110] Ibid. [111] K. E., interview, 2017.

[112] BBC News, "J. K. Rowling outs Dumbledore as gay," October 20, 2007, http://news.bbc.co.uk/2/hi/7053982.stm

[113] L. Camacci, "What counts as Harry Potter canon?" *In Media Res: A Media Commons Project*, November 20, 2016, http://mediacommons.org/imr/2016/11/10/what-counts-harry-potter-canon

Complicating the Fanon

While Camacci describes all fan-related content as fanon, there are distinctions within it as well. According to Goodman, who adds examples to Busse and Hellekson's 2006 definitions:[114]

> "Canon" refers to the original text(s) and their contribution to the fictional universe; it is canon that Harry Potter discovered he was a wizard on his eleventh birthday, as described in *Harry Potter and the Philosopher's Stone*. "Fanon" describes "the events created by the fan community in a particular fandom and repeated pervasively throughout the fantext [body of fan creations]. Fanon often creates particular details or character readings even though canon does not fully support it – or, at times, outright contradicts it."[115]

Certain fan sites, such as MuggleNet and The Leaky Cauldron, which were both supported by J. K. Rowling via occasional in-site interviews and as winners of Rowling's Fan Site Awards (described later herein), served to both construct and police the *Harry Potter* fanon, in particular as far as relationships within were concerned. The "Shipping Wars," "a term that describes the ferocious (and, in some senses, ongoing) debate about whether Hermione was in love with Harry or Ron,"[116] promoted heteronormative relationships. MuggleNet owner Emerson Spartz maintained a "Wall of Shame" within the site, which "consisted of a series of excerpts from the forums [including of alternative relationships] with his sarcastic responses to each, thus creating a conglomerate of toxic fan practices."[117] While MuggleNet and The Leaky Cauldron represented a type of external

---

[114] K. Busse and K. Hellekson, *Fan Fiction and Fan Communities in the Age of the Internet: New Essays* (Jefferson, NC, and London: McFarland & Company, 2006).

[115] Goodman, "Disappointing fans," 667.

[116] S. S. Walton, "The leaky canon: Constructing and policing heteronormativity in the Harry Potter fandom," *Journal of Audience & Reception Studies* 15 (2018), 232.

[117] Walton, "Leaky canon," 244.

policing of the fanon, there was internal monitoring as well, for example, via the fan writing community's own *Harry Potter* fanon wiki.[118] Hamilton and Sefel[119] argue that *Harry Potter* fans have a real sense of co-ownership of Rowling's Potterverse, that they "do not sit passively by as the storyline is sold to them" via either the books or the films, and that, instead, they "take responsibility for its creation."[120]

One big difference between *Harry Potter* fandom and earlier fandoms, such as that of *Star Trek*, is that fans are actually able to communicate with the (original) author via social media:

> I think that's kind of what we have to keep in mind as we're moving forward with fandom is that if they're going to interact with the creators in this brave new world, um, which I think is, is something that has definitely changed because you can tweet at J. K. Rowling.[121]

Referring to the famous debate between Roland Barthes in his essay "Death of the Author"[122] and Michael Foucault in his 1969 response, "What Is an Author?", Moran writes: "Both Barthes and Foucault, then, are criticizing not so much the common-sense notion that individual authors write texts, but the kinds of mystical associations which cluster around them in capitalist societies, naturalizing them as the only authoritative source of textual meaning and as a locus of power and authority within a culture."[123] Barthes's and Foucault's debate about authorship takes on new meaning in Rowling's case. The openness of the world allows fans to borrow, reinvent, reinterpret, and claim as their own elements of the stories, and the "fanon"

---

[118] The Harry Potter fanon can be accessed at http://harrypotterfanon.wikia.com /wiki/Main_Page

[119] H. E. Hamilton and J. M. Sefel, "We are book eight: Secrets to the success of the Harry Potter Alliance," in L. S. Brenner (ed.), *Playing Harry Potter: Essays and Interviews on Fandom and Performance* (Jefferson, NC: McFarland, 2015), 211.

[120] Ibid.

[121] K. E., interview, 2017.

[122] Barthes, *Image, Music, Text*.

[123] Moran, *Star Authors*, 59.

established around her work becomes a point of contention as fans revise and correct and thereby claim ownership of the content.

Many years after all the books and movies were released, one might believe that the online *Harry Potter* fan fiction writing communities would start to disappear, but instead it seems that this fan community has joined the ranks of other long-lasting fan communities, such as *Star Trek*'s. As one writer said (about the *Harry Potter* community surviving the end of the series):

> Um, it slowed down a little but honestly not as much as I thought it would. The stories for [*Harry Potter*] fan fiction are just getting . . . more creative.[124]

In 2017, Caroline Carpenter, acting children's editor for *The Bookseller* and a self-proclaimed "huge fan" of the *Harry Potter* books, felt that the associated fandom overall had been declining slightly in the United Kingdom, but argued that there is much that contributes to keeping the series alive, such as the LeakyCon fan conference, the Warner Bros. Studio Tour London, and the 2017–2018 British Library exhibit. In addition are the books related to the original series, such as *The Cursed Child*, which was the fastest-selling book in nine years (after *Harry Potter and the Deathly Hallows*) when it was published in July 2016, and the best-selling book of the year in the UK the year it was released. The 2016 screenplay of *Fantastic Beasts and Where to Find Them* sold 413,158 copies in one year and special "house editions" of the books also help to keep the series alive. The Jim Kay-illustrated *Harry Potter and the Philosopher's Stone* (2015) sold 170,189 copies in two years, and his illustrated *Harry Potter and the Chamber of Secrets* (2016) sold 98,163 copies in just one year.[125]

When asked if current North Americans are reading *Harry Potter* books as much as those in the same age bracket fifteen or twenty years ago, a librarian answered: "Yes, they're still reading them. There are a lot of

[124] K. W., interview, 2017.
[125] Sales figures were provided by Caroline Carpenter of *The Bookseller* in an interview on October 25, 2017.

times where kids will come up to me and I'll go to the shelf and all our copies are checked out."[126]

Meta-fandom

Harry Potter fan fiction writing is expanding along with new technological innovations. In 2017, Botnick Studies used predictive text keyboards trained on all seven books in the *Harry Potter* series to write an algorithmically constructed *Harry Potter* fan fic. "For the Harry Potter project, specifically, dozens of people were able to use the predictive keyboard and submit their creations to Botnik. Some of the best sentences were chosen by an editor and compiled into the physical chapter":[127]

> "Voldemort, you're a very bad and mean wizard," Harry savagely said. Hermione nodded encouragingly. The tall Death Eater was wearing a shirt that said "*Hermione Has Forgotten How To Dance,*" so Hermione dipped his face in mud. Ron threw a wand at Voldemort and everyone applauded. Ron smiled. Ron reached for his wand slowly.
>
> "Ron's the handsome one," muttered Harry as he reluctantly reached for his . . ."[128]

Stories like this are not great literature in any context, but fans would recognize the content. As Liao wrote in The Verge.com: "The end result is a tale with a plot that feels soulless and meandering but like any good fanfiction, still holds a faint imprint of Rowling's usual lilting whimsical charm."[129] Fans were highly entertained. The original tweet from Botnik

---

[126] K. W., interview, 2017.

[127] K. Beck, "A hilarious new Harry Potter chapter was written by a predictive keyboard – and it's perfect," *Mashable*, December 12, 2017, https://mashable.com/2017/12/12/harry-potter-predictive-chapter/#wPCEiwDL0aqd

[128] Botnik, *Harry Potter* [Predictive text], 2017, https://botnik.org/content/harry-potter.html

[129] S. Liao, "This Harry Potter AI-generated fanfiction is remarkably good," *The Verge*, December 12, 2017, www.theverge.com/2017/12/12/16768582/harry

went viral, with 42,000 tweets in two days,[130] and of course fan art quickly emerged to illustrate the text.

Literary Celebrity, Branded Author

In addition to fans contributing to the success of the series, we must also acknowledge the role of the author's celebrity status. While Rowling's literary celebrity status is complicated as a children's author, her status as a best-selling author made her the first female novelist on the Forbes Billionaires list. But in 2013, she became a member of Forbes's "Billionaire Dropoff" list when she "dropped" to millionaire status because of the amount of wealth she gave away.[131]

Moran writes that "authors can no longer be seen as separate from their public images in a mediatized world,"[132] and indeed, Rowling's public persona, or what we get to see of her, has become a character that affects fans nearly as much as the characters she invented. As a person and as an author, Rowling exists in the ultimate mediatized realm, in which her persona is carefully constructed by narratives presented across media channels. In an era in which the line between public and private lives of celebrities – including celebrity authors – is blurred, and access to an author is associated with the authenticity of the text, Moran's 2000 work is useful in establishing Rowling as a literary star who fiercely guards her private life.[133] Access to Rowling is limited in part because her fame is so stratospheric. Her website discourages attempts to establish a dialogue with her:

PRESS AND PUBLICITY[134]

Do get in touch with any press or publicity enquiries, but please note that J. K. Rowling very rarely gives media

---

[130] A. Menta, "Absurd new 'Harry Potter' book written by predictive text already has fan art," *Newsweek*, December 14, 2017, www.newsweek.com/new-harry-potter-book-written-predictive-text-already-has-fan-art-748331

[131] "Forbes' billionaire list: JK Rowling drops from billionaire to millionaire due to charitable giving," *Huffington Post*, December 13, 2013, www.huffingtonpost.com/2016/12/13/forbes-billionaire-list-rowling_n_1347176.html

[132] Moran, *Star Authors*, 74. [133] Ibid.

[134] Retrieved from www.jkrowling.com/enquiries/

interviews or comment, preferring to make any public comment via Twitter. As a general rule, she does not undertake public speaking or conference engagements.

Because of the huge volume of requests coming in, J. K. Rowling also regrets she is unable to:

- Answer individual questions or comment on specific topics from readers
- Read or comment on writing, stories, ideas or artwork
- Sign copies of books for individuals
- Send out autographs or signed photographs, or personal messages
- Respond to individual requests for financial assistance

Rowling's few public appearances are limited and carefully scripted. Stephenson describes her background story as Rowling's "mythology."[135] Her hero's journey as constructed in the media, from struggling single mother on welfare, writing by hand on a legal pad in an Edinburgh café with her infant daughter at her side, to best-selling writer and one of the world's richest and most charitable women, is as much a part of the *Harry Potter* narrative as the books themselves, and one with which fans everywhere are familiar. Ohlsson, Forslid, and Steiner describe the role of "personalities" that are connected to and help market such products.[136] The visibility of Rowling is key, and her celebrity certainly contributes to the popularity of her work and its adaptations. While she is portrayed as being private, and even somewhat shy, Rowling's limited media engagements attract a rock star welcome. For example, at a book signing and reading in Los Angeles in October, 2007, about 1,600 children appeared in costume. "'This is an amazing treat for me,' Rowling said of the mass book signing and reading for cheering Harry Potter fans who gave her a pop star welcome in Los Angeles."[137]

[135] Stephenson, "Construction of authorship," 57.

[136] A. Ohlsson et al., "Literary celebrity reconsidered," *Celebrity Studies*, 5 (2014), 3.

[137] J. Serjeant, "J. K. Rowling launches U.S. book tour with mass signing," Reuters, October 15, 2007, www.reuters.com/article/us-usa-rowling/j-k-rowling-launches-u-s-book-tour-with-mass-signing-idUSN1537267520071015

Moran argues that the media narrative that is constructed around Rowling is how literary celebrity functions and points out that literary celebrity now applies to how we treat celebrities in general – by reifying individuals and packaging them as ideal archetypes. As such, they serve as marketing tools of the products they represent. Rowling, too, is packaged as an ideal type – beautiful, rich, successful, and extremely generous. This is not to say that Rowling is not in control of her brand. In fact, as an author, Rowling has been able to wield unusual and impressive control over the *Harry Potter* franchise. One example lies with the official Pottermore fan site. Amazon buyers wishing to purchase ebook versions of the books are actually not able to buy them on Amazon. Instead, from Amazon, they are redirected to the proprietary Pottermore site. As a result, Amazon receives a significantly reduced fee. This is not simply about Rowling generating extra profit from sales of the ebooks, but also about how the books can be used and shared. When purchased through the Pottermore site, the ebooks are available without digital rights management, which means that readers can read across multiple devices, and that "the ebooks will also become available to borrow from libraries – for free."[138]

In recent years, Rowling's appearances have been tied to charitable causes – in part to raise money, but also to prevent bookstores and other commercial entities from profiting from ticket sales to her appearances. Restrictions placed on fan online content and on festivals represent a need for crowd control, and also suggest that Rowling (and her corporate partners) are wary of others profiting from *Harry Potter* (as will be further discussed in the section on festivals). And indeed, the control allows Rowling to channel the money as she sees fit – usually to charitable causes, as one fan noted:

> Jo's tour stands out because, in addition to making all of our dreams come true, she'll also be raising money for various charitable causes. Although exact prices have yet to be

---

[138] P. Jones, "How Pottermore cast an ebook spell over Amazon," *The Guardian*, March 28, 2012, www.theguardian.com/books/booksblog/2012/mar/28/pot termore-ebook-amazon-harry-potter

> released, it is being reported that access to Jo's signing lines
> will be granted in exchange for donations to charities local to
> the communities where she'll be holding her events.[139]

Rowling is not the only writer to seek such control. A description of Rowling's 2016 tour on MuggleNet points out that media star and best-selling author Neil Gaiman has had to make similar arrangements.[140] Rowling is very much present through her work and even the spin-off projects. While her physical presence is elusive and limited, she has a virtual presence on Pottermore and Twitter. For many, Twitter is a site of bullying and lawlessness, but for Rowling, Twitter represents a safe, computer-mediated space, and has become a means of communicating with both fans and detractors.

Religion

J. K. Rowling's generosity boosts her status from celebrity to something more of the rank of a religious leader,[141] which connects to her messages of morality (or even spirituality) within the books themselves. Ommundsen describes the difficulty of theorizing "comparisons of systems of religious worship and fan culture," in which Frow's 1995 construction of the celebrity is always dead, and therefore immortal.[142] In contrast, Rowling is very much a living celebrity, who connects with "the religious, or quasi-religious nature of celebrity culture."[143] First of all, Rowling frequently cites the Bible and C. S. Lewis's *Narnia* books, which are infused with Christian themes, as influences on her work.[144] Second, within the *Harry Potter* books,

[139] Jessica J., "Rowling announces 2016 worldwide signing tour," Mugglenet, April 1, 2015, www.mugglenet.com/2015/04/j-k-rowling-announces-2016-worldwide-signing-tour/

[140] Ibid.

[141] J. Granger, *Looking for God in Harry Potter* (Carol Stream, IL: Tyndale House, 2006).

[142] Ommundsen, "Sex, soap," 54. [143] Ibid.

[144] C. McGrath, "The Narnia skirmishes," *New York Times*, November 13, 2005, www.nytimes.com/2005/11/13/movies/the-narnia-skirmishes.html

moral values, and the triumph of good over evil, prevail, which is in line with much religious thought. And finally, Rowling's own charitable acts connect to religious ideals of generosity, sacrifice, and the importance of helping others. Ironically, despite its morality, some religious institutions have condemned the *Harry Potter* series for its content related to magic and witchcraft. Some Christian, Muslim, and Jewish institutions have banned *Harry Potter*.[145] Shortly after publication of the last book in the series, in 2006, the American Library Association was already calling the series the most challenged books of the twenty-first century,[146] and certainly nothing has surpassed them yet.

From Heteronomous-Autonomous to Autonomous-Heteronomous

Books for young people typically rank far lower on the cultural capital scale than books for adults. But anything related to books by J. K. Rowling is an exception. According to *The Bookseller*, the British Library sold 30,000 advance tickets, the greatest number in its history, to its high-culture-meets-pop-culture exhibit, "A History of Magic."[147] The exhibit featured a combination of original manuscripts donated by J. K. Rowling and her British publisher, Bloomsbury, and treasures from the British Library, such as "the Ripley Scroll, a six metre-long manuscript that describes how to make the Philosopher's Stone," the tombstone of Nicholas Flamel, and other magical artifacts, "from mermaids to crystal balls, from broomsticks to garden gnomes."[148] The exhibit included a range of activities and

---

[145] For a complete discussion of religious debates around Harry Potter, see https://en.wikipedia.org/wiki/Religious_debates_over_the_Harry_Potter_series

[146] American Library Association, "Harry Potter tops list of most challenged books of 21st century" [press release], September 21, 2006, www.ala.org/Template .cfm?Section=archive&template=/contentmanagement/contentdisplay.cfm& ContentID=138540

[147] C. Carpenter, "A sneak peek at the British Library's Harry Potter exhibition," *The Bookseller*, October 19, 2017, www.thebookseller.com/booknews/harry-potter-british-library-exhibition-657271</u>

[148] Ibid.

workshops, including courses for adults the catalog described as being "on a range of themes including Witchcraft in Medieval and Early Modern Europe, magical illustration and fantasy fiction."[149] The fact that the exhibit specifically had many events targeting adult interests demonstrates that organizers knew their audience, and distinguishes this event as it filled a gap in the *Harry Potter* marketplace. The British Library exhibit was composed of existing and borrowed items, as is done for exhibits about *Alice in Wonderland* by Lewis Carroll, books by Rudyard Kipling, A. A. Milne's *Winnie-the-Pooh*, and works by J. R. R. Tolkien. Being in such company is indicative of *Harry Potter*'s status in the Western canon of children's literature. And J. K. Rowling, too, belongs among the ranks of literary celebrities, because even though she is a genre author, the *Harry Potter* books are considered to be among the best works of fantasy to date.

The next section focuses on online fan activity.

2 Fans' Shaping of Participation: From Fan Sites to Pottermore

Potter fans have been many in number, fiercely loyal, and highly vocal, especially online.[150] Publication of the *Harry Potter* books coincided with the beginning of Internet chat-rooms and websites, and around the turn of the twenty-first century, individually created, independent *Harry Potter* websites proliferated. J. K. Rowling and Warner Bros. have had an evolving relationship with fans, fan sites, and fan fiction. As Murray wrote in 2004,

> Warner Bros.' changing strategies for managing the global *Harry Potter* fan base and its emotional "ownership" of the *Harry Potter* brand constitute an intriguing case study of a media corporation wrestling with conflicting legal and marketing priorities. It evinces a conglomerate compromised by the need to police its expensively acquired [intellectual property] while at the same time cultivating an international

[149] Ibid.

[150] Portions of this chapter are derived from Martens, *Publishers*.

fan base devoted to the brand, though doubtful of Warner Bros.' commercial motivation.[151]

Fan Resistance

Rowling and Warner Bros. did not initially embrace fan sites.[152] In 1998, after paying a seven-figure price for film and merchandising rights for the first two books in the series, Warner trademarked the *Harry Potter* name, and began to issue cease-and-desist letters to registered domain names that were directly derived from content in the series, such as the famous example of Claire Field, whose website, www.harrypotterguide.co.uk, was the subject of a lawsuit in December 2000.[153]

Another was the *Daily Prophet* online newsletter, started by teenager Heather Lawver. When sued, Lawver organized fans in a counterstrike, boycotting Potter merchandise in conjunction with the release of one of the films in the series.[154] What became known as the PotterWar in the United Kingdom and Defense Against the Dark Arts in the United States had begun.[155] As critic Frank Rose describes:

> The PotterWar . . . pitted Warner Bros. against a citizen's army of web-savvy kids. The movie studio was eager to protect the trademarks it had bought from Rowling; the kids were outraged that a giant corporation was threatening them with legal action for using the Potter name on websites they'd set up to celebrate the story. (Rose 2011)

According to Fanlore.org: "And it worked. Warner Bros lost so much money during the boycott that they retracted the letters and allowed people

---

[151] Murray, "'Celebrating the story'," 14. [152] Ibid.

[153] A. Vickers, "Warner Bros. in fresh battle over Harry Potter website," *The Guardian*, January 22, 2001, www.theguardian.com/media/2001/jan/22/newmedia1

[154] M. Dargis and O. Scott, "The fans own the magic," *New York Times*, July 1, 2011, www.nytimes.com/2011/07/03/movies/the-fans-are-all-right-for-harry-potter.html

[155] Murray, "'Celebrating the story'," 15.

to continue using the copyrighted words and phrases. PotterWar was a big win for the people and set a precedent, giving more freedom to what people could do online."[156]

By 2004, Rowling (and by extension Warner Bros.) had clearly recognized that fans provided important word-of-mouth, peer-to-peer marketing that had supported the success of the series, and that most fan activity would not be a potentially plagiarizing nuisance that might dilute or unfairly profit from the brand. Subsequently, she revised her stance on online fandom, and in acknowledgment of the value of collaborations between fans and content owners, she established the J. K. Rowling Fan Site Award on jkrowling.com. Fan Site Award winners received a crest they could display on their sites as a seal of approval, or badge of recognition. Among the award winners in 2004 was school librarian Steve Vander Ark's *Harry Potter Lexicon* website. The site's announcement stated:

> We were delighted and a bit stunned to discover that the Lexicon was chosen by Jo to receive her Fan Site Award. I can't even tell you what an honor it is to know that Jo actually visits the Lexicon every so often while writing her books, using the site for research. All of us here on staff at the Lexicon were thrilled – okay, we were a little bit past "thrilled." More like delirious.[157]

In 2007 Rowling brought a lawsuit against RDR Books, Steve Vander Ark's publisher, for publishing a print version of the *Harry Potter Lexicon* based on his eponymous website. A New York City court agreed, and the judge blocked its publication. Two years later, in 2009, Vander Ark was able to publish a revised (significantly shortened) version. His website, however, continues.

---

[156] Fanlore.org, "PotterWar," 2015.

[157] S. Vander Ark, "Fan site award," *The Harry Potter Lexicon*, July 1, 2004, www .hp-lexicon.org/author/steve-vanderark/

Why do Fans Write Fan Fiction?

François wrote in 2007 that young authors participate in fan fiction because fan fiction is a major part of the transmedia universe in which they already reside, and for the opportunities afforded for interaction with other readers.[158] According to Goodman, fan fiction provides fans with an opportunity to correct – or even to chastise – an author.[159] But others, such as one fan fiction writer interviewed, described moving on to fan fiction as "a natural progression" after she read the sixth *Harry Potter* book. For her, writing fan fiction provided continuity for her and others like her, who simply "want[ed] more."[160] K. E. described the impatience she and others felt while waiting two years for *Harry Potter and the Deathly Hallows* to be published, and how fan fiction helped to fill the time. She was still a child when she started writing fan fiction, but she mentioned that in the fan fiction community she had interacted with many older fans, some of whom assured her they'd been writing fan fiction since before she was born.

The world created in the series lends itself exceptionally well to story expansions by fans. Yet, as with fan sites, Rowling has not always embraced *Harry Potter* fan fiction. Rowling's lawyers have sent threatening letters to fan fiction writers who include sexually explicit material in their stories.[161] Later, many of the individual fan sites began to disappear as their creators grew up and moved on. Others grew into larger fan sites, many of which support advertising, such as MuggleNet, The Leaky Cauldron, Hogwarts is Here, and Pottermoreforum.net.

MuggleNet

MuggleNet[162] was started in 1999 as an independent fan site by then twelve-year-old Emerson Spartz. The site is now owned by Spartz's media

---

[158] S. François, "Les fanfictions, nouveau lieu d'expression de soi pour la jeunesse?" [FanFiction – A new method of self-expression for youth?], *Agora Débat Jeunesses*, 4 (2007), 58–68.

[159] Goodman,"Disappointing fans," 662–676. [160] K. E., interview, 2017.

[161] N. Walter, "Works in progress," *The Guardian*, October 26, 2004, www.theguardian.com/books/2004/oct/27/technology.news

[162] www.mugglenet.com/

company, DOSE Media Inc. According to a 2015 article in *New Yorker*, Spartz is known as the "King of Clickbait."[163] Using *Harry Potter*, he created many viral posts on MuggleNet, and DOSE Media continues the practice. MuggleNet is profitable because of its in-site advertising, and early on, it was condoned by J. K. Rowling, who not only awarded then eighteen-year-old Spartz with a Fan Site Award in 2004, but also invited him to her home.

The Leaky Cauldron

The Leaky Cauldron website[164] is run by Melissa Anelli, author of the 2008 book *Harry, A History: The True Story of a Boy Wizard, His Fans, and Life Inside the Harry Potter Phenomenon*, to which J. K. Rowling contributed an introduction. Anelli has been working on The Leaky Cauldron since 2001, when she was twenty-one. The website had existed largely separate from the corporations that own *Harry Potter*, but Anelli convinced Warner Bros. and Scholastic to provide reportable information that she could share on the site. Anelli has served as board president of the Harry Potter Alliance and codirector of the LeakyCon Festival, and even served as a consultant on Pottermore. She also visited J. K. Rowling at her home after winning a Fan Site Award in 2005.

While, as the site's disclaimer notes, "The Leaky Cauldron is not associated with J. K. Rowling, Warner Bros., or any of the individuals or companies associated with producing and publishing *Harry Potter* books and films," the organization has managed to effectively collaborate with Warner Bros. and J. K. Rowling, albeit indirectly. The site features information about upcoming events related to the series and sponsored advertising. According to the Leaky site, J. K. Rowling called Leaky her "favorite fan site." Like MuggleNet, The Leaky Cauldron is staffed primarily by volunteers, but it is for-profit, earning money from advertising. Before the launch of Pottermore: The Digital Heart of the Wizarding World,[165] which is now

---

[163] A. Marantz, "The virologist: How a young entrepreneur built an empire by repackaging memes," *New Yorker*, January 5, 2015, www.newyorker.com/maga zine/2015/01/05/virologist

[164] www.the-leaky-cauldron.org/   [165] www.pottermore.com

the official *Harry Potter* fan site, according to the Internet Archive's Wayback Machine (IAWM), Rowling debuted her own "official" news-sharing site, jkrowling.com, in 2000. According to the IAWM in 2018, its peak years of activity were between 2004 and 2005.[166] By April 2018 the most recent news update, informing visitors about J. K. Rowling receiving Britain's Companion of Honour medal, was well over four months old, which is ancient in an era of instant Twitter news updates.

The terms of use posted on jkrowling.com leave a door cracked for fan appropriation. They say that fans may share links for personal, non-commercial purposes only, and that reproducing or publishing any of the content on the site will require written permission. According to the terms of use:

> In some limited circumstances, the Company may choose to permit the reproduction or publication of content where it feels that this does not harm the business or its values and does not negatively affect J. K. Rowling, Warner Bros. Ent., the *Harry Potter*, Fantastic Beasts and/or Pottermore brands (and the Company's decision on this shall be final).[167]

The site further bars readers from using content for commercial purposes, editing it, or removing copyright and proprietary notices associated with it. The notice concludes, "J. K. Rowling's status (and that of any identified contributors) as the author of the content on the site must always be acknowledged."[168] This means that if someone has an idea for the next big fan site, theoretically they might be able to collaborate with the corporate owners.

Pottermore

Pottermore was founded as J. K. Rowling's official *Harry Potter* fan site in 2011. Jointly owned with Warner Bros., it is the mother ship of *Harry Potter*

---

[166] Internet Archive Wayback Machine, jkrowling.com, 2018, https://web.archive.org/web/20050801000000*/http://jkrowling.com

[167] jkrowling.com, "Terms of use," 2018, www.jkrowling.com/tcs/ [168] Ibid.

fan sites and serves as the authoritative source for all things related to the author, the series, and the extension products, as well as for new writings by J. K. Rowling. Readership of Pottermore relies both on the established fame of the *Harry Potter* series and on the celebrity status of J. K. Rowling, whose involvement attracts fans, by providing access to unpublished material on the site, from backstories about the Potter family to writings about the (much-criticized) North American version of Hogwarts, the Ilvermorny School of Witchcraft and Wizardry.

Because they draw on and generalize Native American traditions, the Ilvermorny stories have received much criticism for appropriation across social media – from Salon[169] to Reddit. As one fan fiction writer said: "And um, a lot of her American fans became kind of disenchanted because I think even if they were able to . . . really criticize her view of Native Americans . . . I think there's just kind of this fundamental misunderstanding of how America would work."[170] Allison Mills lays out several of the key problems in Rowling's story in her 2016 article in *The Looking Glass*, from the way she treated "the many Indigenous nations in North America as one monolithic group," to Rowling's "overwriting" of Navajo religion, for example, by claiming that "Skinwalkers" did not exist. Further, Rowling implied that "Medicine People" were frauds, when in reality, while their role varies from nation to nation, "in general Medicine Men and Women serve as healers, educators, and cultural consultants."[171] For Indigenous fans of the series, according to Mills, "when something is meaningful to you and suddenly starts perpetuating the same kind of hurtful stereotypes that your people and culture have been subject to for years, it hurts. Magic in North America is tone deaf. It continues a long history of colonial texts

---

[169] L. P. Young, "Pottermore problems: Scholars and writers call foul on J. K. Rowling's North American magic," *Salon*, July 1, 2016, www.salon.com /2016/07/01/pottermore_problems_scholars_and_writers_call_fou l_on_j_k_rowlings_north_american_magic/

[170] K. E., interview, 2017.

[171] A. Mills, "Colonialism in wizarding America: JK Rowling's history of magic in North America through an Indigenous lens," *The Looking Glass: New Perspectives on Children's Literature*, 19 (2016), para. 5.

which ignore that Indigenous peoples still exist."[172] As of this writing, J. K. Rowling has neither apologized for, revised, nor retracted her work on Ilvermorny.

The original, pre-2015 Pottermore site allowed in-site fan participation. Fans could read the latest news, play games, get sorted into the houses of Hogwarts, and communicate with each other. This idea of being "sorted" and belonging is one that aligns with contemporary YA literature especially (such as the "districts" in Suzanne Collins's *The Hunger Games*), and with high school culture in general.[173] The site gave fan activity a Rowling-centered, carefully controlled, and confined space, and provided communication with fans. While fans may have found that the original site struck a balance between fan agency and corporate control, allowing fans the opportunity to join groups and interact with others within the site, as well as with corporate-produced content, only made the site owners' efforts to moderate bullying and prevent inappropriate content increasingly complicated.

Later, the site owners conducted an analysis of the original Pottermore site and found that users were primarily accessing it using mobile devices rather than desktop computers.[174] Site owners disabled fan participation in April 2015, and then relaunched the site on September 22, 2015. The redesigned site shifted to mobile platforms for non-linear reading, eliminated gaming – including the very popular Sorting Hat feature – and disabled comments. It also shifted focus from the youngest readers of the series to those older readers who had grown up with the books. Games and other participatory elements were replaced with additional backstories, information about the Potters, and news about the latest *Potter*-related products. As the relaunched Pottermore site becomes increasingly commercial and focused on the larger *Harry Potter* franchise, "[v]iewing Pottermore as paracontent is useful for understanding how the website blurs

---

[172] Mills, "Colonialism," para. 10.

[173] K. Waldman, "Everyone knows where they belong," *Slate*, March 21, 2014, www.slate.com/articles/arts/culturebox/2014/03/divergent_harry_potter_and_ya_fiction_s_desire_for_self_categorization.html

[174] P. Jones, "Pottermore readies radical relaunch," *The Bookseller*, September 10, 2015, www.thebookseller.com/news/pottermore-readies-radical-relaunch-312036

the lines between an immersive social platform and a marketing exercise that is subservient to its original texts: the *Potter* books."[175] In fact, a "continued association with author (and authority) figure J. K. Rowling" makes the increasing promotional role of the site "more palatable."[176] In addition, Rowling's authority as creator of the original series is established across the franchise, with the books serving as "one cornerstone of not only the franchise's past but its future as well"[177] as they are linked to new products, from the *Fantastic Beasts* movies to the *Cursed Child* play. Since its 2015 relaunch, very few options for fan interaction limits the site to being one lengthy advertisement for all things Rowling and *Harry Potter* (old and new), in part robbing participants of the full community experience, which subsequently has migrated beyond the walls of the site to social media.

After the original version was taken down, a beta member described how she felt: "I didn't have a way to contact anybody. It was kind of like a real moment of loss."[178] Since they could no longer communicate in-site, fans took to social media to continue the conversation.

Wrath of the Fans

Fans' anger at the redesign was swift, and using hashtag conversations on Twitter around #Pottermore and #BringBackTheOldPottermore, they expressed their dismay. By September 24, 2015, more than 5,000 related tweets had appeared from around the world in English, Spanish, French, Portuguese, and Russian. Initial, close readings of Twitter following these hashtags clearly demonstrated fans' displeasure. Later, my colleague Emad Khazraee used the Personal Zombie application to search Twitter for #Pottermore. This resulted in a data set of 7,062 tweets between September 14, 2015 and October 2, 2015. Tweets were then categorized around the themes that emerged.[179] While some fans defended the change, fans who were displeased felt robbed. They had created potions, earned

---

[175] C. Brummitt, "Pottermore: Transmedia storytelling and authorship in Harry Potter," *Midwest Quarterly*, 58 (2016), 117.

[176] Brummitt, "Pottermore," 113. [177] Ibid., 127. [178] K. E., interview, 2017.

[179] This will be described in detail in an in-progress journal article.

badges, and obtained house memberships through the site and all were gone. Others described feeling that they had been expelled from Hogwarts.

The conflict is a microcosm of the ongoing conflict between media property owners' desire for control and fans' interest in open participation. While fan sites provide a unique lens on fans' tastes, the price of that is a great potential for misbehavior that could damage the property. Site owners must balance their desire for information about fans with a strategy that protects their intellectual property. Shortly after the relaunch, the Pottermore Correspondent was established to address some of the potentially damaging comments on social media, and offered consolations and promises that eventually, users would grow to love the new site even more. The Pottermore Correspondent bridges corporate control with fan agency. By pushing fans' comments outside the Pottermore site and onto social media platforms, site owners do not have to worry about moderating their site. Fans can be free to express themselves in any way they choose, as long as it is not within the site. Having the Pottermore Correspondent acknowledge and address negative comments from social media provides a sense of authenticity, showing fans that at least some comments are noted. After fans complained about the loss of popular items such as the Sorting Hat, in January 2016 the Sorting Hat and wand selection were brought back. In order to promote both the return of the Sorting Hat and the *Cursed Child* play, which had its premiere in June 2016, celebrities and fans took the Sorting Hat quiz to see in which house they belonged. As fans were re-sorted, they were not necessarily pleased with the new results, which often differed from their initial sorts. Fans who had once been Gryffindors or Ravenclaws were dismayed to find that they had been re-sorted as members of Slytherin. Other fans, such as Stevie Weevie D, were upset that they were now Hufflepuffs:

> I took the Pottermore test and good news! I'm a Hufflepuff too! Oh wait that's horrible news Damnit.[180]

---

[180] Stevie Weevie D [@Stoxen42], "I took the Pottermore test and good news!," Twitter, May 26, 2016, https://twitter.com/search?q=I%20took%20the% 20Pottermore%20test%20and%20good%20news!%20I%27m%20a%20Hufflepuff

Often, fans are unhappy at being sorted as Hufflepuffs, and perhaps this stems from the first book. When Hagrid is filling Harry in on Hogwarts culture, he insultingly refers to Hufflepuffs as "a lot o' duffers."[181] However, perhaps this is because Hufflepuffs have been maligned for being "nice," compared to, for example, Gryffindors, who have the much more admirable trait of being "brave."[182] Yet across media platforms, many defend Hufflepuffs, from fans on Twitter, to a 2015 article in *The Atlantic*, in which David Sims says that Hufflepuffs should get more credit for their "strong loyalty, disinterest in public glory, and a hardworking spirit."[183]

Thus, the tension between corporate ownership and fans continues in a new sphere: Pottermore versus social media. As seen in Figure 3, the popularity of the Pottermore site, fueled by information about new releases such as *The Cursed Child* and the *Fantastic Beasts* movies, ebbs and flows according to activity within the franchise. It peaked in early 2018, declined over the summer, and then towards November, when *Fantastic Beasts: The Crimes of Grindelwald*[184] was released, there was another spike in activity. In April 2018, Pottermore.com had a global popularity rank of 7,509 among websites – but on November 26, 2018, it had jumped to 5,671 in the rankings. Pottermore.com quickly eclipsed J. K. Rowling's personal site, perhaps because fans are more interested in the world of *Harry Potter* and any related stories, and slightly less interested in the author J. K. Rowling. The site jkrowling.com had a November 2018 rank of 219,085 (i.e., not very popular at all).

By expressing themselves on social media forums beyond the walls of the corporate-owned site, fans are able to exert pressure on corporate owners

%20too!%20%20%20Oh%20wait%20that%27s%20horrible%20news%20Damnit .&src=typd

[181] J. K. Rowling, *Harry Potter and the Sorcerer's Stone* (New York: Scholastic, 1998).

[182] A. Clarke, "What your Hogwarts house says about you," *Odyssey Online*, 2016, www.theodysseyonline.com/hogwarts-house

[183] D. Sims, "In defense of Hufflepuff," *The Atlantic*, September 18, 2015, www .theatlantic.com/entertainment/archive/2015/09/hufflepuff-rules/405937/

[184] IMDb, "Fantastic Beasts: The Crimes of Grindelwald," 2018, www.imdb.com /title/tt4123430/

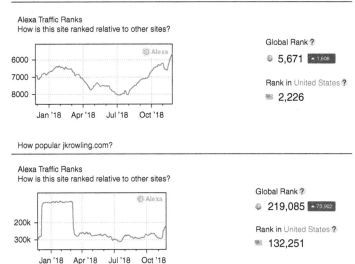

How popular is pottermore.com?

Alexa Traffic Ranks
How is this site ranked relative to other sites?

Global Rank ?
5,671 ▲ 1,608

Rank in United States ?
2,226

How popular jkrowling.com?

Alexa Traffic Ranks
How is this site ranked relative to other sites?

Global Rank ?
219,085 ▲ 73,902

Rank in United States ?
132,251

Figure 3 Popularity of Pottermore.com versus jkrowling.com, as shown on Alexa Internet, Inc. (November 2018)

and actively shape their own online experience. Participating in a site such as Pottermore becomes a negotiated experience for fans and corporate owners. With in-site communication disabled on the Pottermore site, fans can use social media, such as Twitter, as a tool for protest. Of course such protest works two ways – fans can communicate their displeasure with content or features, and the author in turn, can scold fans. But corporate owners are wise to listen to – and negotiate with fans, or they risk losing them entirely.

While online fandoms create community and interactive experiences, fans seeking a more immersive, live experience can visit commercial venues, such as Warner Bros. Studios in London or Universal Studios in Orlando, or they can seek more geographically favorable and affordable venues, such as community-organized Harry Potter festivals, which will be discussed in the next section. As of this writing, as with independent fan sites, Rowling and Warner Bros. are increasingly seeking to control these venues in order to protect their copyrighted content, but here too, Harry Potter fans are resistant to playing by rules imposed on them by corporate owners, especially when such rules interfere with their desire to create their own fan experiences. No matter what the rules are, fans reserve the right to dress up as characters from the books, play Quidditch, and drink Butterbeer.

3 Potterfests

Potterfests are part literary festival, part pop culture festival. Like both of these types of events, they provide a physical, mimetic, and immersive fan experience. Thus, the bodies of literature on both literary festivals and on pop culture festivals provide a foundation for my theorization of locally organized Harry Potter festivals. Harry Potter festivals and events occur internationally and locally, from mass reading events, such as the Harry Potter Book Nights organized by Bloomsbury UK,[185] to hundreds of library events such as Potter Faire Akron.[186] This monograph focuses specifically on two cases – one festival in Kent, Ohio, and the other in Odense, Denmark. The sections below explore these related streams of research.

Literary Festivals: from Live to Digital and Back
From online environments to festivals, "Live experiences bear greater symbolic capital than mediated ones because of the social construction of the performance as valuable."[187]

---

[185] Bloomsbury, "Harry Potter Book Night," n.d., https://harrypotter .bloomsbury.com/uk/harry-potter-book-night/

[186] Akron-Summit County Public Library, "Potter Faire Akron," 2018, www .akronlibrary.org/library-programs/potter-faire-akron

[187] A. Gilbert, "Live from Hall H: Fan/producer symbiosis at San Diego Comic-Con," in J. Gray, C. Sandvoss, and C. L. Harrington, eds., *Fandom: Identities and Communities in a Mediated World*, 2nd edn. (New York: New York University Press, 2017), 362.

Murray and Weber describe contemporary writers' festivals that have added digital components, from a live-feed broadcast of an author's "performance" at a live festival, as in their example of Arundhati Roy's 2004 lecture at the University of Sydney, or the Sydney Writers' Festival live streaming to "libraries and writers' centres in other New South Wales cities and regions," or participation in writers' festivals via a live Twitter feed.[188] Murray and Weber (2017) describe limits to audience participation in cases where it essentially amounts to labor, with organizers requesting "best photos, tweets, quotes, blogposts etc. about the festival to be picked up and recirculated through the festival's official channels."[189]

In contrast, at live Potter festivals, audience participation is as much a part of the festival as anything the organizers construct, and is essential to the success of the event. While organizers provide space, vendors, and entertainment, the participation of large numbers of costumed fans playing Wizard Chess and Quidditch, while quaffing Butterbeer and eating Chocolate Frogs, is what contributes to the success of the festival. Literary festivals typically provide a community of like-minded individuals with access to celebrity authors, but regionally organized Harry Potter festivals do not offer access to J. K. Rowling. It would be prohibitively expensive to provide the logistics and organization such a celebrity would require, as participants at such festivals well understand. And actually, attendance by Rowling at *Potter* festivals is neither expected nor needed. Instead, fans seek "access to a group of strangers with interests compatible with their own."[190] In fact, one fan interviewed, K. W., said that regarding Rowling's presence (or lack thereof), "the magic is ... with the fans, not with her."[191] Fabricated connections with characters, settings, and activities from the books is enough to establish

---

[188] S. Murray and M. Weber, "'Live and local'? The significance of digital media for writers' festivals," *Convergence: The International Journal of New Media Technologies*, 23 (2017), 64.

[189] Murray and Weber, "'Live and local'?" 71–72.

[190] Murray and Weber, "Live and local'?" 70. [191] K. W., interview, 2017.

the type of community connections that Driscoll describes,[192] which in turn help reinforce the bonds among *Harry Potter* fans attending the festival. Thus, community feeling, which Ommundsen describes as "a powerful motivation for [literary] festival participants,"[193] plays a far greater role for *Potter* festival attendees than author–fan interaction. Online extensions of such festivals do occur on social media, as participants post pictures on Facebook and Instagram before and after the event, but the primary focus of the festival is live. *Potter* festivals serve as an opportunity for fans – who may or may not participate in other online fan sites – to express their love of the series in a community of like-minded individuals.

Compared to book fairs, which have been around since the Middle Ages, literary festivals are a relatively recent phenomena within the arena of book history. In her 2018 book *Literary Festivals and Contemporary Book Culture*, Millicent Weber states that there are currently "450 literary festivals held annually across the English speaking world."[194] The oldest, the Cheltenham Literature Festival, started in 1949 and sells approximately 215,000 tickets a year.[195] Examples of similar festivals exist internationally, such as the Adelaide [Australia] Writers' Week, held since 1960, the Hay Festival of Literature and the Arts, held annually in Wales since 1988, and festivals in Aarhus, Denmark; Cartagena, Columbia; Jaipur, India; and Brooklyn, New York.

By taking what is normally a solitary experience, reading, and making it a public, social, collective event, as Ommundsen says:

> Literary festivals ... differ from festivals devoted to other
> art forms such as cinema, music and other performance arts,
> which simply offer a more concentrated experience of the
> normal mode of consumption ... Festivals are the visible

---

[192] B. Driscoll, "Sentiment analysis and the literary festival audience," *Continuum: Journal of Media & Cultural Studies*, 29 (2015), 861–873.

[193] Ommundsen, "Literary festivals," 29. [194] Weber, *Literary Festivals*, 4.

[195] Cheltenham Literature Festival, "About," n.d., www.cheltenhamfestivals.com /about/key-facts-and-timeline/

and public manifestations of an art form that is highly invisible and private.[196]

At literary festivals, it is common for authors to perform readings of their work or to engage in discussions relating to it, providing audiences with experiences similar to attending a musical or theatrical performance. Just like fan sites, literary festivals provide readers with access to authors they love, while simultaneously revealing the audience to the authors and their publishers. While Ommundsen describes "physical proximity with the author" as an important component that attracts audiences to literary festivals, this is not the case with *Potter* festivals around the world.[197] Literary festivals also provide authors and their publishers with information about fans.

Driscoll writes that "[e]ngagements with literary culture are not simply intellectual, but also personal, intimate, and emotional."[198] She calls festivals a sort of "intimate public sphere." Certainly, it is difficult to call the experience of attending Kent's Potterfest with more than 20,000 other fans "intimate," but festivalgoers still experience a sense of belonging to a larger *Harry Potter* community, which fans describe as being a key part of *Harry Potter* fandom, however it is created. Weber describes "the social" as an "essential element of the literary festival's appeal," pointing out that festivals provide an opportunity to engage face-to-face with other like-minded individuals.[199]

Local *Potter* festivals are related to formalized media events, such as Comic-Con. Comic-Con started in San Diego in 1970 with 100 attendees and currently hosts more than 130,000 attendees each year.[200] Open to industry professionals and to the public, it is both a fan event and a marketing event, as there are many possibilities for fans to participate, but also for marketers to advertise new and existing properties to its fanbase. Here, participatory fandom serves as a way to promote business and

[196] Ommundsen, "Literary festivals," 21. [197] Ibid.
[198] Driscoll, "Sentiment analysis," 861. [199] Weber, "Conceptualizing," 91.
[200] Comic-Con, "About," 2018, www.comic-con.org/about

consumption.[201] Gilbert describes fans' attendance at Comic-Con as a type of "pilgrimage" performed by fans "into a media world that occupies a space of industry commerce and promotion."[202] Because they are independently run and not commercially organized, Potterfests represent a far less structured environment than Comic-Con – but also lack its free merchandise.

In contrast to elaborate and commercially organized events like Comic-Con, amateur Potterfests such as the one in Kent, Ohio, are often free of charge. These events give fans an indirect connection to the object of their fandom. For some fans, attending a festival may represent a sort of pilgrimage, just as Gilbert described with Comic-Con above. While they are non-commercial, volunteer-driven, and completely dependent upon fans' contributory participation, they still depend on the goodwill of Warner Bros. Commercial aspects of amateur festivals may inadvertently violate copyright, but for Warner Bros., doggedly pursuing such copyright infringement could present potentially devastating public relations consequences, particularly in an era in which it is easy to disseminate complaints via social media. Warner Bros. has recently sent cease-and-desist letters to some amateur organizers in the United States,[203] but as of this writing they had not taken further legal action – although that might change quickly.[204] For example, there were at least eighteen independently organized *Harry Potter*-inspired festivals in 2017 in the United States alone, with many more

---

[201] Gilbert, "Live from Hall H," 355. [202] Gilbert, "Live from Hall H," 357.

[203] Michelle Sahr, interview with the author, September 6, 2017; A. Hoover, "N.J. Harry Potter-themed festival shut down by movie studio who must-not-be-named," NJ.com, November 21, 2018, www.nj.com/gloucester

[204] In addition to the Kent Potter Fest organizers receiving a cease-and-desist letter from Warner, during 2017 and 2018, other fairs too have received these letters, and this has been covered by the media: C. Chaplain, "Warner Bros. sparks outrage after crackdown on Harry Potter fan events to 'preserve trademark,'" *Evening Standard*, June 16, 2018, www.standard.co.uk/news/world/warner-bros-sparks-outrage-after-crackdown-on-harry-potter-fan-events-to-preserve-trademark-a3864721.html; "Warner Bros. casts cease-and-desists letters to curse Harry Potter fan festivals," *Daily News*, June 16, 2018, www.nydailynews.com/entertainment/ny-warner-bros-harry-potter-festival-crackdown-20180616-story.html

events held at public libraries. Other festivals include Ireland's LeakyCon, one in Edmonton, Alberta, Canada, and the Harry Potter Festival in Odense, Denmark, which I will discuss later herein. Bridging the space between Comic-Con-type fan events and literary festivals, organizers of these amateur festivals seek to create affordable, family-friendly events with strong connections to reading. Reviews by festivalgoers, such as one who attended the 2017 Potterfest in Kent, Ohio, from a nearby city, described the festival as a "little staycation" for their family on the event's Facebook page. Indeed, locally organized Harry Potter festivals, which are free of charge or inexpensive to attend, present an inclusive and affordable way for families to participate in face-to-face fandom without an expensive trip to Harry Potter World in Florida.

These events featured a range of activities, from scholarly talks, to family-style cosplay and games, to pub crawls. Examples are described in Table 2.

Attendance figures from Table 2 were reported either on festivals' websites, on social media, or in local media, and in a few cases, conference organizers were contacted for further information. An "adult" audience means that the event was held in a venue that served alcohol, which in the United States means that attendees must be over 21, the legal age for consuming alcohol, whereas an event for a "general" audience had activities for children and families. Where the audience is specified as "academic," there was a focus on research.[205]

While many of these events targeted families, others included activities that specifically addressed the 20-to-30-year-old *Harry Potter* Generation. For example, a New York City nightclub hosted the March 2017 Webster Hall event, which restricted attendance to participants over the age of twenty-one. Similarly, Atlanta's Potter Pub Crawl and Wizard's Ball in November 2017 was an adult-themed event for those 18 and older (or 21 and older to participate in the Potter Pub Crawl). This event, which has been held since 2014, offers activities such as wand-making and Butterbeer-

---

[205] A spreadsheet demonstrating how data was collected is available at https://docs .google.com/spreadsheets/d/1ACk38GaRJYckySXX20MDhdwNIMuITlvP6 FrmUaAaUR0/edit?usp=sharing

Table 2 2017 North American Potterfests

Name of event	Location	Date	Cost of attending	Audience focus	Estimated attendance
Wizard Fest	Webster Hall, New York	March 18	$15–$25	Adult	Unknown
Atlanta's Potter Pub Crawl and Wizard's Ball	Atlanta, GA	November	$20–$40	Adult	Unknown
Roanoke Harry Potter Festival	Roanoke, VA	May 13	$5–$10	General	8,000
Kent's Potterfest	Kent, OH	July 29	Free (pay-as-you-go for activities)	General	22,000
Spellbound Festival	St. Bonaventure University, St. Bonaventure, NY	August	$200 (for conference)	Academic	Unknown
Harry Potter Arts and Curiosities Festival (and pub crawl)	Sunbury, PA	September 9	Free ($10 for drink specials at local bars)	General	Unknown
Chestertown Harry Potter Festival	Chestertown, MD	October 6–7	$15–$20	General	5,000+
The Harry Potter Festival 2017	Chestnut Hill, PA	October 20–21	Free (pay-as-you-go for activities)	Academic and general	45,000
Harry Potter Festival USA	Jefferson, WI	October	$15–$25	General	42,000

drinking. Perhaps in an attempt to avoid attention from Warner Bros., the Atlanta pub crawl thinly disguised the names of the houses of Hogwarts: "Grifendor" instead of "Gryffindor," "Rayvenklaw" for "Ravenclaw," "Slitheryn" for "Slytherin" and "Huhfullpuff" for "Hufflepuff."

On the other hand, the Roanoke Harry Potter Festival in Virginia was aimed at general audiences, including families, with Harry-Potter-themed games, events, and food. Attendees could participate in Wizard Chess, make wands, attend potions classes, and play Quidditch. They could shop at Diagon Alley-style stores for magical items or dine with food vendors serving high tea and Butterbeer. Other events had more of an adult or academic theme, from scholarly talks to specialty cocktails, beer gardens, and pub crawls, and provided significant high cultural connections, as suited to a literary event, via scholarly talks.

Chestnut Hill's Harry Potter Weekend advertised that "Potter fans of all ages can enjoy an enchanting weekend of film screenings, sorting hat demonstrations, a scavenger hunt and more."[206] In addition to the family-friendly activities, Chestnut Hill's festival also had activities with definite adult appeal: "On Friday evening, hit up places like The Night Kitchen, serving up butterscotch beer with shots of firebolt (Fireball whiskey) and eats such as golden frog iced brownies and pulled pork sliders." There were also two local beer gardens where fans could enjoy sudsy "potions al fresco."

The Spellbound Festival held at St. Bonaventure University in New York State in August 2017 was free to the public, but room and board cost $200. This festival combined an academic, scholarly conference, including talks such as "*Harry Potter* and the Feminist Conundrum," with fan experiences such as shopping in Diagon Alley, participating in live-action Wizard's Chess, or taking an herbology class, which again approaches the autonomous-heteronomous sphere.

Acknowledging copyright law, several festival organizers held in 2017 posted disclaimers on their websites:[207]

---

[206] Visitphilly.com, "Harry Potter festival in Chestnut Hill," n.d., www.visitphilly.com/events/philadelphia/harry-potter-weekend-in-chestnut-hill/

[207] Months after these festivals were held, some of the links no longer work.

Sunbury Harry Potter Arts and Curiosities Festival: "We are in no way affiliated or supported by the wonderful J. K. Rowling and we hope that no one sends us to azkaban" [sic].[208]

Chestertown Harry Potter Festival: "The Chestertown Harry Potter Festival is a fan-created non-profit event to celebrate the spirit and theme of *Harry Potter* and promote our local community and its arts. Warner Bros. Entertainment and J. K. Rowling are not associated with or responsible for the festival in any way."[209]

Roanoke Harry Potter Fest: "The Roanoke Harry Potter Fest is an immersive celebration of the magical world. It is not endorsed, sanctioned or in any way affiliated directly or indirectly with J. K. Rowling, Warner Brother Studios Entertainment, Publishers or their representatives."[210]

The Roanoke festival organizers may have received a warning from Warner Bros., as in 2018 the festival's site announced: "The festival which must not be named: The Roanoke Harry Potter Festival is happy to announce that we shall henceforth be known as Diagon Valley. We are excited to bring the magic back to the Roanoke area on October 6, 2018!"[211] In June 2018, the link to the former Roanoke Harry Potter Festival, renamed "Diagon Valley" in early 2018, had changed its name once again, this time to "The Generic Magic Festival." According to the site, "The copyright holders of our previous name have sent us a Cease and Desist letter, exercising their right and duty to protect their art and characters. We have decided to shift our festival to celebrate all literary magic, and decided a slightly tongue-in-cheek name would be a fun nod at [the] absurdity of our situation."[212] Further, under the "Vendors" tab, the

[208] Little Studio Big Art, "Harry Potter festival," 2013, www.littlestudiobigart.com /harry-potter-fest

[209] Chestertown HP Festival, 2016, https://chestertownHarry Potterfest.org/

[210] Roanoke Harry Potter Festival, n.d., www.roanokepotterfest.com/meet-us/

[211] https://diagonvalley.org/

[212] Generic Magic Festival [Roanoke, VA], n.d., www.genericmagicfestival.com/

festival organizers make it clear that "Generic Magical Festival can only allow vendors who agree to follow the federal and state laws regarding copyrights. We strongly recommend avoiding all terms coined by JK Rowling or other artists."[213] The Chestnut Hill Harry Potter Festival changed its name in 2018 to the Chestnut Hill Harry Potter Conference and Festival, emphasizing the academic nature of the event.

Scott Cramer, one of the organizers of the Jefferson, Wisconsin, Harry Potter Festival, told the *Daily Jefferson County Union* that they had heard from Warner Bros. through its attorney that "the festivals are getting way out of hand," and that the festival would "give people the feeling of the *Harry Potter* experience without utilizing any of the proper names [from the book]." Diagon Alley and Knockturn Alley were thus renamed "Dragon's Alley" and "Serpent's Alley."[214] As of this writing, another festival in New Jersey, the Pitman Potter Festival, had been renamed the Pitman-Festival-That-Must-Not-Be-Named.[215] While festival organizers might not be experts in copyright and trademark law, and even believe that they are promoting the franchise via their activities, when they receive correspondence from Warner Bros. they realize the potential problem of being sued by such a powerful media entity.

Kent's Potterfest

Kent, Ohio, is a city of about 32,000 people and is home to Kent State University. During the academic year, the population of the city doubles. Kent's Potterfest was first planned as a book release party for *Harry Potter and the Cursed Child* at a local toy store, but other community partners, including shops and the library, got involved based on interest through word of mouth and social media, primarily Facebook. Main Street Kent, a non-profit organization focused on the revitalization of Kent's downtown, took over planning the event and has continued to plan it annually. The first Potterfest, held in summer 2016, attracted approximately 10,000 people.

---

[213] Ibid.

[214] A. Zoellner, "Fans, vendors updated on Potter Fest," *Daily Union*, April 4, 2017, www.dailyunion.com/news/article_fef6b16e-2121-11e7-b583-3769de21fe58.html

[215] Hoover, "N .J. Harry Potter-themed festival."

Based on the enormous success of the 2016 event, a more formal committee was formed for 2017. Planning started nine months before the July 29 festival. From stores to cafés to restaurants to the library, both individuals and organizations in the town participated in the festival, and it was widely advertised and promoted on social media, especially Facebook. Because of this community engagement with a mass-market product, festivals such as Kent's represent a heteronomous-autonomous (see Figure 2) engagement with the *Harry Potter* franchise.

According to one of the organizers, Michelle Sahr, the committee grew nervous about potential attendance when Facebook "likes" crossed the 20,000 mark in anticipation of Kent's second Potterfest. The Only in Your State website described the event as "a 'Harry Potter Wonderland.'"[216] The event gained more than 22,000 likes on its Facebook group (which as of May 2018 had been removed), and after the festival the local paper, the *Record Courier*, estimated the number of attendees at 20,000. This success had its costs, as will be seen in the next section.

Conflict with Warner Bros.

According to the *Record Courier*, Kent's Potterfest began to draw national attention when it was listed on the Only in Your State website. "As people from outside northeast Ohio began to learn about the event, so did officials at Warner Bros."[217] About two months before the festival, the organizers, Main Street Kent, received a cease-and-desist letter from Warner Bros.[218] Organizers ultimately obtained permission to proceed in 2017 if they followed a series of rules laid out by Warner. It appears that Warner Bros. conceded to allow the 2017 event to go forward largely because it was already in progress and canceling it would have been upsetting to fans who had already made plans to attend. One of Warner Bros.'s rules in 2017 was that only public spaces could be named after areas in the books. Accordingly, Kent's Acorn Alley became Diagon Alley (Figure 4), and the Dan Smith Park became the Forbidden Forest.

[216] D. Smith, "Potterfest summons throngs to Kent," *Record Courier*, August 1, 2017, 1.

[217] Smith, "Potterfest summons," 2.

[218] Michelle Sahr, interview with the author, September 6, 2017.

Figure 4 Kent's Acorn Alley, renamed Diagon Alley

Anything with commercial, or perceived-commercial connections, would not be allowed to use copyrighted names. For example, temporarily renaming the local toy store, Off the Wagon, as "Weasley's Wizard Wheezes" would not be acceptable, despite the fact that the items of greatest interest were the licensed *Harry Potter* merchandise, which sold out the night before Potterfest. Shops around Kent were not allowed to sell their own versions of branded items, although Facebook comments and eyewitness accounts suggest that locations in town did sell their own interpretations of Butterbeer.

Other changes to the festival reflected the growing attendance. For example, while there had been costume judging the first year, in 2017 there was none, as organizers felt there would be too many people. But many participants did not need any motivation to engage in cosplay (Figure 5).

Kent's Potterfest included plenty of free, do-it-yourself activities, such as the "Wanted" posters shown in Figure 6, which visitors could borrow free of charge for portraits:

Figure 5 Cosplay fans dressed as Hagrid, Luna Lovegood, and Hermione

Figure 5 (cont.)

Figure 5 (cont.)

Figure 6 Make-your-own "Wanted" poster

Other activities required a fee, including the Horcrux Hunt and Wizard Chess. Reflecting Rowling's personal commitment to children's charities, Warner Bros. required Main Street Kent to gain sponsorship for the event from a children's charity, and to donate a portion of the proceeds to such charity; thus, activity fees went to local charities such as Birdie Bags (a charity that distributes weekend backpacks of food and clothing to children in need in Kent). This is perhaps a continuation of the moral guidance inherent in the books, and the organizers embraced Warner Bros.'s requirement.

Kent Free Library made book displays for the event (see Figure 7), held an activity modeled on the Restricted Section of the library at Hogwarts, and invited a local wildlife organization to host multiple owl presentations, which could be attended free of charge, via sign-up. Unfortunately, there were not nearly enough shows to accommodate the number of people interested in attending.

Under Warner Bros.'s rules, stores that were either vacant or closed on the day of Potterfest could be decorated with signs inspired by the books (Figure 9), since these stores would not benefit commercially from the

Figure 7 Kent Free Public Library book recommendations from book characters

Figure 7 (cont.)

Figure 8 Acceptable magical retail venue: a vendor set up a creative shop that sold unlicensed "magical" items that could have been in the books

Figure 9 Faux shops

Figure 9 (cont.)

festival. Other vendors offered unlicensed "magical" goods for sale (Figure 8).

The handmade signs provide evidence of the community-wide dedication and effort that went into the festival.

Analysis of Social Media Comments

Post-festival, there were many comments on the Kent Potterfest Facebook page.[219] A content analysis of the posts revealed the following themes: travel and crowds, copyright and legal issues, activities for adults, and love for the event, as described below.

Travel and Crowds

The term "pilgrimage" could be applied to fans who travel to visit both commercial and non-commercial *Harry Potter* venues. According to Merriam-Webster, a pilgrimage is "a journey of a pilgrim; *especially*: one to a shrine or a sacred place."[220] Katherine Larsen describes the *Harry Potter* fan pilgrimage to sites including Platform 9¾ at King's Cross Station in London, Warner Bros. Studio Tour London, and Universal Studios Orlando.[221] While Kent's festival drew many from the state of Ohio, some participants traveled a considerable distance to attend. Participants, who might not have been able to afford a trip to England or to Orlando, Florida, described lengthy car trips from states including Indiana, Michigan, New York, Pennsylvania, Vermont (over ten hours away by car), West Virginia, and one poster who described driving eight hours to attend from Tennessee. Some had booked rooms in local hotels so they could arrive the night before. Another family described camping nearby. Even Ohioans traveled as much as four hours from cities across the state, such as Cincinnati. The discomfort of travel, and then of navigating the crowds, could symbolize sacrifices (within family budgets) made in line with their devotion to the books.

[219] Comments discussed here are from July 28 through August 2, 2017.

[220] Merriam-Webster, "Pilgrimage," 2018, www.merriam-webster.com/diction ary/pilgrimage

[221] K. Larsen, "(Re)Claiming Harry Potter fan pilgrimage sites," in L. S. Brenner (ed.), *Playing Harry Potter: Essays and Interviews on Fandom and Performance* (Jefferson, NC: McFarland, 2015).

While there were enthusiastic comments throughout the Facebook page, there were also many complaints, and overcrowding was the biggest source of anger. Some attendees were upset that they had been unable to see shows, such as the owl show at the library. Other commenters complained that overcrowding contributed to dangerous situations with traffic, highlighting a lack of signs, police officers, or even volunteers to direct traffic. One attendee wrote, "We began to feel instant remorse the second we pulled into town." Another felt that Kent was simply too small to hold the number of people who had attended, describing being trapped in a sea of people. One commenter claimed to have witnessed a traffic accident involving a pedestrian (which was not verified). A self-described first responder noted a lack of first aid stands and police presence and thought more streets should have been closed to traffic. Participants such as Kristen Radilovic Swinehart were annoyed that lines to buy anything from Butterbeer to *Harry Potter*-themed merchandise were as long as they are at amusement parks:

> [I]t was so crowded you could not see or do anything. The vendors had run out of product by the time we could even see them. There were lines for the events like we were at Cedar Point [a popular amusement park in Ohio].[222]

There were also comments expressing annoyance that the toy store had sold all of its licensed merchandise the night before the festival began. Several suggested that there should be more merchandise and Butterbeer, and more places to buy both. For example, festivalgoer Lydia Flowers described a general lack: "Not enough bathrooms, not enough vendors, not enough events, not enough Butterbeer."[223] And everyone definitely wanted to buy Butterbeer. Festivalgoer Susan Meadows finally had to give up: "We

[222] K. R. Swinehart, Kent Potterfest 2017 Facebook group. www.facebook.com /events/376920692675541/?active_tab=discussion

[223] L. Flowers, Kent Potterfest 2017 Facebook group. www.facebook.com/events/ 376920692675541/?active_tab=discussion

attempted to stand in line for Butterbeer but gave up when the line didn't move an inch in over 20 minutes."[224]

Another commenter, Adam Cramer, took a more realistic approach, chastising complainers:

> [Festival organizers] put on a great event, Was it crowded? Yes, Long lines to do most things? Yes. But what do people expect from the world of *Harry Potter*. It's mostly a free event for family's [sic] to come out and enjoy the atmosphere with other Potterheads in a small college town. Haters will always find something to complain about. Seems no one has the patience to wait in lines and enjoy why they are there in the first place.[225]

Aside from those who took to social media to complain, the overcrowding was also reported elsewhere (and observed by the author). An otherwise enthusiastic reviewer writing on July 29, 2017 on OhioFestivals.net stated, "the crowds made it torturous to explore while not knowing where to find anything" and further complained about parking being "a nightmare," and experiencing "huge waits" for food.[226]

Copyright and Legal Issues

Facebook posters were overall either unaware or unconcerned about copyright infringement spotted at the festival, but one festivalgoer, Sarah Kettering, posted that she was "Sad to hear from a cashier that [the festival] won't happen next year because of Warner Bros."[227]

---

[224] S. Meadows, Kent Potterfest 2017 Facebook group, www.facebook.com /events/376920692675541/?active_tab=discussion

[225] A. Cramer, Kent Potterfest 2017 Facebook group, www.facebook.com/events/ 376920692675541/?active_tab=discussion

[226] OhioFestivals.net, "Kent Potterfest review," July 29, 2017, https://ohiofesti vals.net/potterfest/

[227] S. Kettering, Kent Potterfest 2017 Facebook group, www.facebook.com /events/376920692675541/?active_tab=discussion

Activities for Adults

Because *Harry Potter* fans who grew up with the series are now adults
themselves, while Kent's Potterfest was very much advertised as
a family event, appropriate for a general audience, there were some
fans who sought more adult-appropriate activities. Kent is a college
town, which means that many young adult attendees expect locally
organized events to have music and alcohol. Consequently, there were
two overlapping levels of attendees: families with young children, and
fans old enough to consume alcohol (age 21 in the United States). Some
of the bars in town had organized *Harry Potter*-themed cocktails to cater
to this group. This led to some confusion. One poster commented that it
was not clear if the event was for "family" or a "bar crowd." In future
events, the poster suggested, it would make sense to start serving alcohol
at 9 p.m. As an attendee named Sandra Shinn wrote: "Having more
adult-themed attractions would be great as well considering many of us
grew up with [the series] (although I absolutely adore the young HP
fans)." Another individual commented that in order to make the extensive travel required to attend worth their while, it would have made
sense to have more adult-themed events for those traveling more than
two hours.

Love for the Event

Overall, participants were highly positive about their experience due to the
event's local accessibility and affordability. Some, probably unaware that
Warner Bros. would make it difficult to hold another event in precisely the
same style, hoped for a repeat in 2018. In response, the festival organizers
wrote that while they had not determined if the festival would be held in
2018, they loved having magical events in Kent. In January 2018, the *Record
Courier* wrote:

> "It was the best day [we'd] ever had," said [Executive
> Director of Main Street Kent, Heather] Malarcik, of July's
> Potterfest, which is based on the *Harry Potter* novels and
> movies. However, the organization is trying to decide how
> to avoid upsetting Warner Bros., which owns the rights to

the *Harry Potter* films, over possible copyright infringement, she said.[228]

While Malarcik would not share Warner Bros.'s correspondence, which she noted was labeled "not for distribution," she said that the festival organizers, bowing to pressure from Warner Bros., had changed the name of future festivals to the more generic-sounding "Wizardly World of Kent." While they were allowed to in 2017, in 2018 the festival organizers did not use any names from the books. Although the town's Acorn Alley was dubbed "Diagon Alley" in 2017, in 2018 it was named "Dragon Alley." As the next section will describe, Warner Bros. has recently placed restrictions on the Harry Potter Festival in Odense, Denmark, that are similar to those it placed on Main Street Kent.

Harry Potter Festival Odense, Denmark

Librarian Søren Dahl Mortensen[229] has organized an annual Harry Potter Festival in Odense, the birthplace of beloved fairytale author Hans Christian Andersen, since 2001. Whereas festivals such as Kent's are firmly rooted in pop culture, the one in Odense is punctuated with highbrow cultural elements from across the arts – including literature, dance, and music – that elevate its cultural capital.[230] The city's library continues to play a primary role in organizing the festival. Child dancers from Odense's Royal School of Ballet and Theater perform, and Odense's symphony hosts a "Harry Potter Concert," to which it charges approximately the same amount it would cost to go to the movies in Denmark.[231]

The first festival was held in 2001 as a dinner for 200 children seated at long tables in Odense's City Hall, a castle-like, red-brick building completed in the 1880s. The festival quickly became an annual event, with

---

[228] B. Gaetjens, "Main Street Kent looks to continue successful downtown events," *Record Courier*, January 8, 2018, www.record-courier.com/news/20180108/main-street-kent-looks-to-continue-successful-downtown-events

[229] This section is based on an interview with Søren Dahl Mortensen in April 2018.

[230] Bourdieu, *Distinction*.

[231] In 2017, concert tickets cost 120 Danish crowns (approximately US$14).

collaborators from around the city. In addition to the library, the ballet, and the symphony, the art museum and local businesses also participate. According to Dahl Mortensen, J. K. Rowling attended the festival in 2010, when she was in Odense to receive the newly established Hans Christian Andersen Literature Award and fell in love with the city. By October 2017, attendance at what has grown into a three-day festival had increased to approximately 12,500 people. Attending the festival is free, and as with festivals across the United States, many attendees arrive in costume. Galleons are the official currency from the series, and visitors can convert their Danish crowns at "Gringott's Bank." For the price of a few galleons, attendees can participate in creative activities such as making wands, capes, or brooms. Likewise, attractions such as a pop-up "creepy animal shop," where local nature leaders educate audiences about snakes and spiders, can be visited for a fee. Attending an owl show is free but holding an owl costs 600 galleons.[232] Ticket holders can dine Hogwarts-style at long tables in the historic City Hall. Catering also to older fans, the festival has evening activities including pub crawls, cocktails, and cosplay.

Odense's festival is a not-for-profit event, and as of 2017, the festival's budget was 1.3 million Danish crowns.[233] Approximately 500,000 crowns came directly from the city of Odense, with more given by local corporate sponsors, whose names were featured on the program and website. Festival-related expenses include items such as tent rentals, electricity, and security. According to Dahl Mortensen, who remains involved, tent rental, a significant portion of the budget and highly necessary in a rainy country, costs 180,000 Danish crowns. The library supports Mortensen's role as organizer and contributes the time of a graphic designer, who is responsible for designing the professional-looking program, website, promotional material, and festival map, which has to be redrawn each year. Volunteers supply

---

[232] Harry Potter Festival Odense, "Program," 2017, https://harrypotterfestival .dk/sites/harrypotterfestival.dk/files/Harry%20Potter%20Program% 202017_web1.pdf

[233] As of April 24, 2018, 1,300,000 million Danish crowns was about 175,000 euros, 153,000 British pounds, or 213,000 US dollars (www.xe.com/currencyconver ter/convert/?Amount=1300000&From=DKK&To=GBP).

the rest. Chemistry students from the University of Southern Denmark in Odense make elixirs, and Scout troops run a Horcrux Hunt. Dahl Mortensen claims he has so many requests from would-be volunteers that he has to turn some away. As in Kent, Ohio, Warner Bros. required that earnings be donated to various charities, including the local children's hospital, but until recently had not deterred the event in other ways.

As with informal Harry Potter festivals in the United States, volunteer organizations running Odense's festival are not necessarily aware of potential conflicts with copyright holders, and Rowling's visit in 2010 probably created a sense of legitimacy. However, Warner Bros. contacted Mortensen in Fall 2017, advising him that while sponsorship via non-profit organizations, such as the County of Odense (Odense Kommune), are permissible, the festival is no longer allowed to use any corporate sponsorships, which accounted for nearly two-thirds of the 2017 budget. Warner Bros. also requested that the festival limit use of any copyrighted names from the book on local businesses or products. This presented a major problem to the organizers, who in the past had freely used terms, concepts, and themes from the book on the website, in the program, and in the attractions, and local businesses had adopted these terms, concepts, and themes as the festival has grown. What this means for the future of the festival is unclear, but in 2018, the festival officially changed its name to Magiske Dage Odense (Odense's Magical Days).

While the legal status of many festivals is somewhat nebulous, it is also clear that they serve multiple purposes for fans and even, arguably, for the corporate owners. As events, they are local and inexpensive (if not free). By dressing up and showing up, fans have a do-it-yourself way to immerse themselves in the *Harry Potter* fan community at little or no cost, which reifies their love for the series and promotes it to new participants. The live fan experience extends the reading experience, providing a tangible immersion in *Harry Potter* fandom, and represents a transmedia, cross-platform way to participate.

Commodified Participation (Platform 9¾): Warner Bros. Studio Tour London

For those who can afford it, Warner Bros. offers plenty of opportunities for corporate-endorsed, commodified participation. The Wizarding World of

Harry Potter at Universal Studios in Florida and the Warner Bros. Studio Tour London represent examples of fully authorized, corporate-owned fan venues available for fans' participation – at a price. Unlike the festivals, which are available either locally, or at least are reachable via a car, commodified venues generally require airfare and steep admission prices to attend, and are beyond reach for many fans. At local events, fans have some agency in directing the activities. For example, in Kent, fans could opt to engage in cosplay, participate in games, or serve as a vendor or performer. At the corporate-owned sites, which arguably provide an experience closely modeled on the books and movies (the Warner Bros. Studio Tour literally takes place in the studio where all the movies were filmed), fans are provided with a fully heteronomous-heteronomous experience (see Figure 1), where they can physically immerse themselves into commodified landscapes recreating the films, purchase licensed merchandise, and consume Warner Bros.-approved Butterbeer in a souvenir cup. At the Wizarding World of Harry Potter theme park, fans can physically enter Diagon Alley, ride the Hogwarts Express, or enter Gringott's Bank via a wild ride.[234]

Due to the popularity of the series, and the world-building within, it is very easy to commodify nearly anything related to the series. Platform 9¾ at Kings Cross Station in London was once a small tribute to the series – half of a luggage cart fused to a wall in the train station, with a sign identifying it as such, was set up in 1999.[235] On a Wednesday morning in September 2017, the same luggage cart was surrounded by velvet ropes to organize a lengthy line of mostly adult tourists, who waited for professional photographers to take their photograph next to it. Next door was a sizable gift shop featuring branded goods that ranged from expensive leather satchels to t-shirts, scarves, and ties.

---

[234] Universal Theme Park Orlando, "The Wizarding World of Harry Potter," 2018, www.universalorlando.com/web/en/us/things-to-do/rides-attractions/harry-potter-and-the-escape-from-gringotts/index.html

[235] Fodor's, "London's 18 most magical Harry Potter sites," 2018, www.fodors.com/world/europe/england/london/experiences/news/photos/londons-18-most-magical-harry-potter-sites

Clearly, anything associated with J. K. Rowling's *Harry Potter* world has the potential to be enormously lucrative. But amateur Potter festivals allow fans to celebrate their fandom in a community of like-minded individuals without necessarily spending a lot. In reinterpreting and recreating Rowling's world, they extend it beyond what Henry Jenkins refers to as their "living rooms"[236] and into their neighborhoods and communities – thereby sharing ownership in the world – with no author presence required. Whether they are fans for a day or fans every day, their participation serves to propagate the series, keeping it alive for a new generation of readers.

Perhaps inspired by messages in the books, or by J. K. Rowling's own charitable acts, however fans choose to participate, whether it is across fan sites or at physical participatory venues, fandom often takes an activist stance. The next section describes fans who do good works in the name of *Harry Potter*.

4 Fans' Active Volunteering: the Harry Potter Alliance

The Harry Potter Alliance (HPA) provides fans with opportunities to translate their fan participation into social justice and activism.[237] *Harry Potter* activism spans political protest and fandom, as fans use the mechanisms of political protest, such as social media, to shape their fandom and make their voices heard. Founded in 2005, the HPA is a non-profit organization dedicated to working for "equality, human rights, and literacy" and provides fans with an opportunity to extend their *Harry Potter* fandom into a different arena – civic action.[238] Habermas distinguishes between literary and political spheres, but for *Harry Potter* fans, the HPA provides an opportunity to connect their literary love for *Harry Potter* with political activism.[239] Former comedian Andrew Slack cofounded the HPA in 2005 with brothers Joe and Paul DeGeorge, who were both musicians in the band Harry and the Potters. According to HPA Executive Director Matt Maggiacomo, "[Joe] DeGeorge first read the *Harry Potter* novels one summer while in college, when he borrowed the four available at the time

---

[236] Jenkins, *Textual Poachers*. [237] Harry Potter Alliance, "What we do."
[238] Ibid. [239] Habermas, *Structural Transformation*.

from his brother, who was eight years younger. He was struck by how *Harry Potter* seemed anti-authoritarian."[240] As the young characters in the *Harry Potter* series enact change on their own, independent from the adults around them, the HPA, too, encourages action from young people. Through the HPA, *Harry Potter* fans connect their good works to the inherent activism in the books: a celebration of breaking rules when done for good reason; taking action for the greater good; and following your own best instincts. The Harry Potter Alliance focuses these energies and, according to its website, it "turns fans into heroes."[241] Through the alliance, *Harry Potter* fandom goes from the screen to real life, as fans become philanthropists and activists for social causes in Harry's name.

As participatory *Harry Potter* readers engage with the brand and contribute to the overall fan experience, their consumption arguably makes them what I call "branded readers."[242] Just as I've described J. K. Rowling earlier as a "branded author," fans of the series constitute a branded readership, linked by their consumption of and participation in the books and related content – as they provide their immaterial and affective labor as peer-to-peer marketers, content creators, participants in festivals, or volunteers serving with an organization that is aligned with the series and its perceived values.

Yet at the same time, *Harry Potter* readers are also very much "empowered consumers."[243] When these fan site creators were facing lawsuits about fan site domain names, they organized a boycott against *Potter* merchandise (PotterWar). When the Pottermore site was redesigned, unhappy fans launched a Twitter revolt to protest the changes. The Harry Potter

---

[240] J. Weiss, "Harry Potter becomes best-selling book series in history with more than 500 million copies sold worldwide," Syfy Wire, February 2, 2018, www .syfy.com/syfywire/harry-potter-becomes-best-selling-book-series-in-history -with-more-than-500-million-copies

[241] Harry Potter Alliance Facebook page, n.d., www.facebook.com/theHarry Potteralliance/

[242] Martens, *Publishers*.

[243] K. Jarrett, "Labor of love: An archaeology of affect as power in e-commerce," *Journal of Sociology*, 39 (2003), 335–351.

Alliance provides a venue both for making positive social change, and also for learning how to be an activist. Live events are coordinated via local chapters, such as one at Kent State University described herein.

According to Fatemi (2018), Generation Z includes those who were born from the mid-1990s to 2010.[244] While it is too early to say what they will accomplish, many members of this generation embrace activism and use social media as their instrument. Often this activism is criticized as being "slacktivism," "[t]he practice of supporting a political or social cause by means such as social media or online petitions, characterized as involving very little effort or commitment."[245] But this might have changed with the "#NeverAgain" movement, which began in early 2018 as a student-led response to the Marjorie Stoneman Douglas High School shooting on February 14, 2018 in Parkland, Florida. These protests in support of gun control and other liberal causes in the US have shown a high level of commitment from teens. While the movement started as an online campaign, it developed into a day of physical protests on March 24, 2018 across the United States. From *Teen Vogue*[246] to CNN,[247] much has been written about how *Harry Potter* has inspired young activists, including the Parkland activists. Nine months after the shooting, Emma Gonzaléz, one of the leaders of the movement, wrote in an op-ed piece in the *New York Times* that she dreams about being able to go back to the time before the shooting. Now that she and fellow students have a new identity as Parkland survivors, Gonazaléz wrote: "All of us know what it feels like to be Harry Potter

[244] F. Fatemi, "What's your strategy for attracting generation Z?" *Forbes*, March 31, 2018, www.forbes.com/sites/falonfatemi/2018/03/31/whats-your-strategy-for-attracting-generation-z/#262703b76cad

[245] Oxford University Press, *Oxford Living Dictionary*, 2018, https://en.oxforddictionaries.com/definition/slacktivism

[246] E. Cerón, "Why 'Harry Potter' means so much to the Parkland activists," *Teen Vogue*, March 26, 2018, www.teenvogue.com/story/what-harry-potter-means-to-parkland-activists

[247] R. Sklar, "Harry Potter inspired the Parkland generation," CNN, March 26, 2018, www.cnn.com/2018/03/26/opinions/parkland-march-harry-potter-generation

now."[248] A teacher, Jennifer Ansbach, tweeted: "I'm not sure why people are so surprised that the students are rising up – we've been feeding them a steady diet of dystopian literature showing teens leading the charge for years."[249] For those in the HPA, a commitment to social justice, as embodied by this movement, is linked to the moral values that the books advance. As Hamilton and Sefel (2015) write, "collective heroism and personal responsibility are two of the benchmark themes of the Potterverse."[250]

Just as fans who engage in fan fiction or festivals seek a sense of community in their participation, working with the HPA provides a similar sense of belonging. As Hamilton and Sefel note, the HPA encourages its members to "think of themselves as 'book eight' in the *Harry Potter* series, responsible for carrying on Rowling's characters' good works."[251] The HPA gives young adult fans a chance to connect with the values inherent in the series in a more mature way, by taking action in causes they believe in.

As of November 2018, there were 426,941 "likes" on the HPA's Facebook page.[252] The HPA offers fans a chance to connect fandom with J. K. Rowling's personal mission of charity as exemplified via her foundation, Lumos. The HPA's idea of the "everyday hero"[253] is borrowed in admiration of Rowling's own work at Amnesty International, but also from the books themselves, in which many characters demonstrate that they are capable of heroic deeds, from Harry, Hermione, and Ron to Luna Lovegood and Neville Longbottom.

Janae Phillips is director of Leadership and Education at the HPA. According to Phillips, the HPA is not affiliated with J. K. Rowling or any of her corporate partners and she has no interaction with the organization. That said, in a 2007 *Time* magazine interview Rowling was pleased with the

---

[248] E. Gonzaléz, "A young activist's advice: Vote, shave your head and cry whenever you need to," *New York Times*, October 5, 2018, www.nytimes.com /2018/10/05/opinion/sunday/emma-gonzalez-parkland.html

[249] L. Miller, "Teens already know how to overthrow the government," *The Cut*, March 16, 2018, www.thecut.com/2018/03/parkland-students-emma-gonzalez

[250] Hamilton and Sefel, "We are book eight," 210. [251] Ibid.

[252] Harry Potter Alliance Facebook page, n.d.

[253] Hamilton and Sefel, "We are book eight," 213.

work of the HPA: "It's incredible, it's humbling, and it's uplifting to see people going out there and doing that in the name of your character."[254] As another indicator of Rowling's approval, in 2007 the HPA received a J. K. Rowling Fan Site Award.[255] While J. K. Rowling does not endorse the HPA for now, the organization has not experienced the kinds of legal action experienced by fan sites and festivals, despite the fact that the website continues to have strong associations with content from the book. If the HPA decided to turn its attention towards criticizing something within the *Harry Potter* community, the chances are good that Warner Bros. would move in with legal action. *Harry Potter* activism is permitted, as long as such activism is about approved causes.

Organization and Activity

According to Phillips, in 2017 there were 230 HPA chapters in the United States, with members ranging in age from 13 to 50, and there are chapters in thirty-eight countries around the world. Phillips notes that the HPA considers itself global, as chapters in Uganda have been involved in building schools, and chapters in South America work with children's hospitals. According to Phillips, the HPA community is young, female, and queer. Most organizers in the US are high school- and college-aged, and the majority (88 percent) are women. About 50 percent of HPA members belong to the LGBTQIA+ community. Despite the heteronormativity of the books, identity exploration is welcomed within the *Harry Potter* fan community in general.

Many local chapters have names inspired by resistance within the books, such as Dumbledore's Army of New Paltz (New York) and Dumbledore's Army: Harnett Battalion (North Carolina). Others include elements from the series, such as Dobby's Defenders (California), L.U.N.A. (Lions United Nerds for Activism, California), Lumos Flashes (Kent, Ohio) and The Weasleys and Extended Family (Reno, Nevada). The HPA has

---

[254] N. Gibbs, "Persons of the year 2007 runners-up J. K. Rowling," *Time*, December 19, 2007, http://content.time.com/time/specials/2007/personofthe year/article/0,28804,1690753_1695388_1695436,00.html

[255] Fanlore.org, "J. K. Rowling Fan Site Award."

worked in support of the Marriage Equality campaign, raised money for Haiti following the 2010 earthquake, lobbied for Net Neutrality, and, most famously, organized the 2008 Not in Harry's Name campaign, which successfully convinced Warner Bros. to switch to a fairtrade chocolate producer for its chocolate frogs.[256]

The HPA's annual conference, the Granger Leadership Academy (GLA), "uses pop culture to make activism accessible,"[257] and attracts approximately 200 participants each year. In 2016 it was held in Warwick, Rhode Island, in 2017 in St. Louis, Missouri, and in 2018 in Tucson, Arizona. As one of the organizers, Phillips considers the GLA to be a condensed version of the Harry Potter Alliance. The GLA allows for authentic, intergenerational fan experience and trains future activists of any age. She explains, "For us, that intergenerational approach is really important for a couple of reasons. One, there're not very many opportunities for adults to be, what we call emerging activists, so if you're a new activist, you're emerging."[258]

Local HPA Chapter: Lumos Flashes, Kent State University

Lumos Flashes, Kent State University's local HPA chapter, was founded in 2015, and like the national HPA, its members mainly identify as women and include many from the LGBTQIA+ community. Beneficiaries of their efforts include a school in Uganda, for which they collected books, the American Heart Association, and the emergency fund of the local LGBTQIA+ group.

C. M., a former president of Lumos Flashes at Kent State, says that the club is committed to social justice first and fandom second.[259] As a self-described member of the *Harry Potter* Generation, C. M. has been a huge fan of the books for most of her life. She started reading the series in first grade and owns three wands – two in the style of Hermione's and Ginny's,

[256] Harry Potter Alliance, "Not in Harry's name," 2015, www.thehpalliance.org /success_stories_nihn

[257] Granger Leadership Academy, "Content," https://grangerleadershipacademy .com/faqs/

[258] J. Phillips, interview, 2017. [259] C. M., interview, 2017.

and one that chose her, a red wand from the Hungarian wand shop at LeakyCon. C. M. was a beta tester of Pottermore; she is among many who feel the original was superior to the redesign of 2015. C. M. also attended the GLA in 2017, and is listed as a sponsor of the 2019 event.

C. M.'s reflections on her involvement in the HPA suggest that its existence mirrors the growing maturity of the Potter generation. Her own desire to make positive change in the world, while maintaining a connection with the fan community she knows and loves, makes activism appealing to her – whether such activism is participating in the Pottermore protests, collecting books for Uganda, or making sure that licensed *Harry Potter* chocolate is ethically sourced and produced. The HPA provides young adult fans with a meaningful way to participate in their fandom, in a community that matches their values – perhaps shaped from multiple readings of the books. As of November 2018, the most recent post on Kent State University's Lumos Flashes Facebook page was from April 30, 2018, which could indicate that the group is now dormant.

Expansion and potential

In 2018, twenty years after the first *Harry Potter* book was published in the United States, and thirteen years after the HPA was founded, the HPA has begun to expand beyond *Harry Potter*-related fandoms and is collaborating with young adult author John Green and shows such as *Steven Universe*, *Voltron*, and *Avatar*. In November 2017, the HPA had six staff members distributed across the United States and five board members, who provided expertise from organizing to banking to legal aid. In November 2018, the staff and board had shrunk slightly, with five staff members and three board members. Whether or not the Harry Potter Alliance will be replaced by new activist organizations such as #NeverAgain is unclear, but arguably, there is a strong connection between *Harry Potter* fandom and activism.

The *Harry Potter* series inspires courageous acts and subversion of authority figures in order to make positive change, and it is not surprising that fans of the series internalize these messages. The activist stance of *Harry Potter* fans is clear, whether they are protesting online about cultural appropriation in Ilvermorny, or the lack of representation in the series; working with and around corporate owners to rename "Potterfests" with titles that do not infringe upon copyright such as The Generic Magic Festival, the Pitman-Festival-That-Must-Not-Be-Named, Magiske Dage Odense, or the Wizardly World of Kent; or directly connecting their fandom to political activism. The fan experience will be on their terms, not as dictated by the corporate owners, and when these experiences are threatened, the community lets its voice be heard.

Conclusion

In 2018, while many members of the *Harry Potter* generation are still very active within multiple dimensions of the fandom, and some are parents themselves, *Harry Potter's* corporate owners (J. K. Rowling and Warner Bros.) must come up with new ways of working with fans to keep the stories alive for future generations – while not estranging them via cease-and-desist letters or lawsuits. From fan sites, to festivals, to fan activism, *Harry Potter* fans are inspired to participate in the *Harry Potter* universe, and their participation contributes to its success – and its longevity, as fans' immaterial and affective labor continues to promote the universe and keep it in the public eye. But often this participation raises questions of ownership and leads to conflict between fans and owners of the copyright and associated trademarks. Fans' labor connects the three arenas presented herein – fans' participation in fan sites and social media, involvement in amateur "Potter" festivals, and engagement with fan activism.

In the cases presented here, fans have an ingrained perception of co-ownership of the series and a sense of agency, as they contribute to creating the fan experiences they desire. Participatory sites serve to uphold the canon, argue against the "meta-canon," or develop the "fanon," but when the possibilities for such interaction are removed, fans migrate toward social media sites such as Twitter on which they are free to express their discontent. Using hashtags, fans can create online communities of dissent, which ultimately can be damaging to the copyrighted and trademarked universe.

Potter festivals exist in the interstices between literary festivals and pop culture events such as comic-cons. Unlike literary festivals, Potter festivals do not require the author's presence; rather, they are about connecting with a community of like-minded individuals. Potter festivals are not quite comic-cons either, as they are not as blatantly commercially-driven and often have free admission. Potter festivals reflect the communities they are in, whether they are hosted in college towns, such as Kent, Ohio, or in cities such as Odense, Denmark. While they are organized by those within the community, they attract fans from afar who are eager to connect with a wider community of *Harry Potter* fans. Such festivals allow fans to engage in their own interpretations of book-inspired activities, from cosplay, to Wizard Chess or Quidditch, to sampling Butterbeer. In doing so, they inadvertently – and often unknowingly – invite legal scrutiny from Warner Bros., which, as of this writing, is increasingly issuing cease-and-desist letters to festival organizers.

Earlier, I discussed Jenkins's[260] view on how fans' participation in cultural commodities contributes to the overall cultural wealth of the community engaging in a particular fandom, and certainly this has been shown in the case studies herein. Jenkins further argues that the circulation of a particular cultural commodity also impacts ownership of such commodity – from reception to social interaction. While my sample sizes here are small, I would argue that fans participating in each of these spheres, from online fan sites, to fan festivals, to fan activism, believe that Harry Potter also belongs – at least a little bit – to them.

The inherent values in the books – the triumph of good over evil – have inspired fan activists and an interest in social justice, from participating in the *Harry Potter* Alliance to joining a movement such as #NeverAgain in the United States. The message of fan agency, personal connection, and authenticity is loud and clear across the sites explored within this Element, and should be acknowledged and respected by the corporate owners above. If Warner Bros.' ultimate goal is to limit fan agency, create "model fans," and control independent fan activity, and instead steer fans toward the approved, commodified sites (which those who can will visit anyway), it seems that ultimately, they will do more damage than good to the brand. *Harry Potter* fans are likely to speak up, resist, and revolt. Forging a path toward coexistence would ultimately benefit both sides, particularly as the franchise – and the fans – age.

---

[260] Jenkins, *Textual Poachers*.

Bibliography

Aaron, M. (2015, November 10). So you haven't seen Star Wars ... A Harry Potter geek's guide to a galaxy far, far away. http://community .sparknotes.com/2015/11/10/so-you-havent-seen-star-wars-a-harry-potter -geeks-guide-to-a-galaxy-far-far-away

Akron-Summit County Public Library (2018). Potter Faire Akron. www .akronlibrary.org/library-programs/potter-faire-akron

American Library Association (2006, September 21). Harry Potter tops list of most challenged books of 21st century [press release]. www.ala.org /Template.cfm?Section=archive&template=/contentmanagement/con tentdisplay.cfm&ContentID=138540

Associated Press (2018, June 16). Warner Bros. casts cease-and-desist letters to curse Harry Potter fan festivals. *Daily News*. www.nydailynews.com /entertainment/ny-warner-bros-harry-potter-festival-crackdown -20180616-story.html

Bacon-Smith, C. (1992). *Enterprising Women: Television Fandom and the Creation of the Popular Myth*. Philadelphia: University of Pennsylvania Press.

Barthes, R. (1977). *Image, Music, Text*. Translated by S. Heath. New York: Hill and Wang.

Baym, N. (2014). Perils and pleasures of tweeting with fans. In K. Weller, A. Bruns, J. Burgess, M. Mahrt, & C. Puschmann, eds., *Twitter and Society*. New York: Peter Lang, pp. 221–36.

BBC News (2007, October 20). J. K. Rowling outs Dumbledore as gay. http://news.bbc.co.uk/2/hi/7053982.stm

Beck, K. (2017, December 12). A hilarious new Harry Potter chapter was written by a predictive keyboard – and it's perfect. *Mashable*. https:// mashable.com/2017/12/12/harry-potterpredictive-chapter

Bennett, L. (2014a). Fan/celebrity interactions and social media: Connectivity and engagement in Lady Gaga fandom. In L. Duits, K. Zwann, & S. Reijnders, eds., *The Ashgate Research Companion to Fan Cultures*. Burlington, VT, and Farnham, UK: Ashgate, pp. 109–20. http://orca.cf.ac.uk/70270/

Bennett, L. (2014b). Tracing textual poachers: Reflections on the development of fan studies and digital fandom. *Journal of Fandom Studies*, 2(1), pp. 5–20. https://doi.org/10.1386/jfs.2.1.5_1

Bennett, L., Chin, B., & Jones, B. (2016). Between ethics, fandom and social media: New trajectories that challenge media producer/fan relations. In A. Davisson & P. Booth, eds., *Controversies in Digital Ethics*. New York: Bloomsbury Academics. www.bloomsbury.com/us/controversies-in-digital-ethics-9781501310546/

Bloomsbury (n.d.). Harry Potter book night. https://harrypotter.bloomsbury.com/uk/harry-potter-book-night/

Booth, P. (2010). *Digital Fandom: New Media Studies*, 1st edn. New York: Peter Lang.

Botnik (2017). *Harry Potter* [predictive text]. https://botnik.org/content/harry-potter.html

Bourdieu, P. (1984). *Distinction: A Social Critique of the Judgement of Taste*. Cambridge, MA: Harvard University Press.

Bourdieu, P. (1993). *The Field of Cultural Production: Essays on Art and Literature*. New York: Cambridge University Press.

Bourdieu, P. (1996). *The Rules of Art: Genesis and Structure of the Literary Field*, 1st edn. Translated by S. Emanuel. Stanford, CA: Stanford University Press.

Bradley, L. (2018, February 15). Fantastic beasts: The crimes of Grindelwald and Dumbledore's vexing sexuality. *Vanity Fair*. www.vanityfair.com/hollywood/2018/11/fantastic-beasts-the-crimes-of-grindelwald-dumbledore-gay-queerbaiting

Brough, M. M., & Shresthova, S. (2011). Fandom meets activism: Rethinking civic and political participation. *Transformative Works and Cultures*, 10. https://journal.transformativeworks.org/index.php/twc/article/view/303

Brummitt, C. (2016). Pottermore: Transmedia storytelling and authorship in Harry Potter. *Midwest Quarterly*, 58(1), pp. 112–32.

Bruns, A., & Highfield, T. (2015). Is Habermas on Twitter? Social media and the public sphere. In C. Christensen, G. Enli, A. Bruns, E. Sokgerbo, & A. O. Larsson, eds., *The Routledge Companion to Social Media and Politics*. New York and Oxford: Routledge, pp. 56–73.

Bruns, A., Moon, B., Paul, A., & Münch, F. (2016). Towards a typology of hashtag publics: A large-scale comparative study of user engagement across trending topics. *Communication Research and Practice*, 2(1), pp. 20–46. https://doi.org/10.1080/22041451.2016.1155328

Busse, K., & Hellekson, K. (2006). *Fan Fiction and Fan Communities in the Age of the Internet: New Essays*. Jefferson, NC, and London: McFarland.

Camacci, L. (2016, November 10). What counts as Harry Potter canon? *In Media Res: A Media Commons Project*. http://mediacommons.org/imr/2016/11/10/what-counts-harry-potter-canon

Carpenter, C. (2017, October 19). A sneak peek at the British Library's Harry Potter exhibition. *The Bookseller*. www.thebookseller.com/booknews/harry-potter-british-library-exhibition-657271

Cerón, E. (2018, March 26). Why "Harry Potter" means so much to the Parkland activists. *Teen Vogue*. www.teenvogue.com/story/what-harry-potter-means-to%09parkland-activists

Chaplain, C. (2018, June 16). Warner Bros. sparks outrage after crackdown on Harry Potter fan events to 'preserve trademark'. *Evening Standard*. www.standard.co.uk/news/world/warner-bros-sparks-outrage-after-crackdown-on-harry-potter-fan-events-to-preserve-trademark-a3864721.html

Cheltenham Literature Festival (n.d.). About. www.cheltenhamfestivals.com/about/key-facts-and-timeline/

Chestertown HP Festival (2016). http://chestertownhpfest.org/

Clark, B. L. (2004). *Kiddie Lit: The Cultural Construction of Children's Literature in America*. Baltimore, MD: John Hopkins University Press.

Clarke, A. (2016). What your Hogwarts house says about you. *Odyssey Online*. www.theodysseyonline.com/hogwarts-house

Collins, J. (2010). *Bring on the Books for Everybody: How Literary Culture Became Popular Culture*. Durham, NC: Duke University Press.

Comic-Con (2018). About. www.comic-con.org/about

Coté, M., Pybus, J. (2007). Learning to immaterial labor 2.0: Myspace and Social Networks. *Ephemera*, 7, pp. 88–106.

Cramer, A. (2017). Kent Potterfest 2017 Facebook group post. www.facebook.com/events/376920692675541/?active_tab=discussion

Dargis, M., & Scott, O. (2011, July 1). The fans own the magic. *New York Times*. www.nytimes.com/2011/07/03/movies/the-fans-are-all-right-for-harry-potter.html

Das, R. (2016). "I've walked this street": Readings of "reality" in British young people's reception of Harry Potter. *Journal of Children and Media*, 10(3), pp. 341–54.

Davenport, T. H., & Beck, J. C. (2002). *The Attention Economy: Understanding the New Currency of Business*, rev. edn. Boston: Harvard Business Review Press.

Driessens, O. (2013). The celebritization of society and culture: Understanding the structural dynamics of celebrity culture. *International Journal of Cultural Studies*, 16(6), pp. 641–57. https://doi.org/10.1177/1367877912459140

Driscoll, B. (2015). Sentiment analysis and the literary festival audience. *Continuum: Journal of Media & Cultural Studies*, 29(6), pp. 861–73.

EdwardTLC (2007, October 20). J. K. Rowling at Carnegie Hall reveals Dumbledore is gay. *Leaky Cauldron*. www.the-leaky-cauldron.org

/2007/10/20/j-k-rowling-at-carnegie-hall-reveals-dumbledore-is-gay-neville-marries-hannah-abbott-and-scores-more

FanFiction.Net (2018). https://fanlore.org/wiki/FanFiction.Net

Fanlore.org (2015). PotterWar. https://fanlore.org/wiki/PotterWar

Fanlore.org (2016). J. K. Rowling Fan Site Award. https://fanlore.org/wiki/J.K._Rowling_Fan_Site_Award

Farr, C. K. (2015). *A Wizard of Their Age: Critical Essays from the Harry Potter Generation*. Albany, NY: State University of New York Press.

Fatemi, F. (2018, March 31). What's your strategy for attracting generation Z? *Forbes*. www.forbes.com/sites/falonfatemi/2018/03/31/whats-your-strategy-for-attracting-generation-z/#262703b76cad

Fiske, J. (2010). *Understanding Popular Culture*. Oxford and New York: Routledge.

Fiske, J. (2011). *Reading the Popular*, 2nd edn. Oxford and New York: Routledge.

Flowers, L. (2017). Kent Potterfest 2017 Facebook group post. www.facebook.com/events/376920692675541/?active_tab=discussion

Fodor's (2018). London's 18 most magical Harry Potter sites. www.fodors.com/world/europe/england/london/experiences/news/photos/londons-18-most-magical-harry-potter-sites

François, S. (2007). Les fanfictions, nouveau lieu d'expression de soi pour la jeunesse? [FanFiction – A new method of self-expression for youth?] *Agora Débat Jeunesses*, 4(46), pp. 58–68. www.cairn.info/revue-agora-debats-jeunesses-2007-4-page-58.htm

Frow, J. (1995). *Cultural Studies and Cultural Value*. Cornell East Asia Series. Oxford: Clarendon Press.

Gaetjens, B. (2018, January 8). Main Street Kent looks to continue successful downtown events. *Record Courier*. www.record-courier.com/news/20180108/main-street-kent-looks-to-continue-successful-downtown-events

Galuszka, P. (2015). New economy of fandom. *Popular Music and Society*, 38(1), pp. 25–43.

Garner, D. (2008, May 1). Ten years later, Harry Potter vanishes from the best-seller list. *New York Times*. https://artsbeat.blogs.nytimes.com /2008/05/01/ten-years-later-harry-potter-vanishes-from-the-best-seller-list/?mcubz=3&_r=0

Generic Magic Festival [Roanoke, VA] (n.d.). www.genericmagicfestival.com/

Gibbs, N. (2007, December 19). Persons of the Year 2007 runners-up J. K. Rowling. *Time*. http://content.time.com/time/specials/2007/per sonoftheyear/article/0,28804,1690753_1695388_1695436,00.html

Gilbert, A. (2017). Live from Hall H: Fan/producer symbiosis at San Diego Comic-Con. In J. Gray, C. Sandvoss, & C. L. Harrington, eds., *Fandom: Identities and Communities in a Mediated World*, 2nd edn. New York: New York University Press, pp. 354–68.

Glass, L. (2004). *Authors Inc.: Literary Celebrity in the Modern United States, 1880–1980*. New York: New York University Press.

González, E. (2018, October 5). A young activist's advice. *New York Times*. www.nytimes.com/2018/10/05/opinion/sunday/emma-gonzalez-parkland.html

Goodman, L. (2015). Disappointing fans: Fandom, fictional theory, and the death of the author. *Journal of Popular Culture*, 48(4), pp. 662–76.

Granger, J. (2006). *Looking for God in Harry Potter*. Carol Stream, IL: Tyndale House.

Granger Leadership Academy (n.d.). Content. FAQ page. https://granger leadershipacademy.com/faqs/

Green, J., Green, H., et al. (n.d.). Crash Course. https://thecrashcourse .com/about

Guerrero-Pico, M. (2017). #Fringe, audiences and fan labor: Twitter activism to save a TV show from cancellation. *International Journal of Communication*, 11, p. 2071–92.

Habermas, J. (1989 [1962]). *The Structural Transformation of the Public Sphere*. Cambridge, MA: MIT Press.

Hamilton, H. E., & Sefel, J. M. (2015). We are book eight: Secrets to the success of the Harry Potter Alliance. In L. S. Brenner, ed., *Playing Harry Potter: Essays and Interviews on Fandom and Performance*. Jefferson, NC: McFarland, pp. 207–19.

Harry Potter Alliance (2015a). Not in Harry's name. www.thehpalliance.org /success_stories_nihn

Harry Potter Alliance (2015b). What we do. www.thehpalliance.org /what_we_do

Harry Potter Alliance Facebook page (n.d.). www.facebook.com /theHarryPotteralliance/

Harry Potter Festival Odense (2017). Program. https://harrypotterfestival .dk/sites/harrypotterfestival.dk/files/Harry%20Potter%20Program% 202017_web1.pdf

Hill, M. (2016, January 12). 16 reasons why Star Wars and Harry Potter are secretly EXACTLY the same: May the "orphan fighting evil with magic pointy sticks" be with you. *Digital Spy*. www.digitalspy.com/movies/ star-wars/feature/a779720/16-reasons-harry-potter-is-just-the-original -star-wars-trilogy-in-new-trousers/

Hills, M. (2013). Fiske's "textual productivity" and digital fandom: Web 2.0 democratization versus fan distinction? *Participations*, 10(1), pp. 130–53.

Hills, M. (2018). Implicit fandom in the fields of theatre, art, and literature: Studying "fans" beyond fan discourses. In P. Booth, ed., *A Companion to Media Fandom and Fan Studies*. New York: John Wiley & Sons.

Hinck, A. (2011). Theorizing a public engagement keystone: Seeing fandom's integral connection to civic engagement through the case of the Harry Potter Alliance. *Transformative Works and Cultures*, 10. https:// doi.org/10.3983/twc.2012.0311

Hoover, A. (2018, November 21). N.J. Harry Potter-themed festival shut down by movie studio who must-not-be-named. *NJ.com*. www.nj.com /gloucester-county/index.ssf/2018/11/nj_harry_potter_festival_ shut_down_warner_bros.html

Huffington Post (2013, December 13). Forbes' billionaire list: JK Rowling drops from billionaire to millionaire due to charitable giving. www .huffingtonpost.com/2016/12/13/forbes-billionaire-list-rowling _n_1347176.html

IMDb (2018). Fantastic Beasts: The Crimes of Grindelwald. www .imdb.com/title/tt4123430/

Internet Archive Wayback Machine (2018). jkrowling.com. https://web .archive.org/web/20050801000000*/http://jkrowling.com

J., Jessica (2015, April 1). Rowling announces 2016 worldwide signing tour. Mugglenet. www.mugglenet.com/2015/04/j-k-rowling-announces -2016-worldwide-signing-tour/

Jaffe, A. (2005). *Modernism and the Culture of Celebrity*, 1st edn. Cambridge: Cambridge University Press.

Jarrett, K. (2003). Labor of love: An archaeology of affect as power in e-commerce. *Journal of Sociology*, 39(4), pp. 335–51.

Jenkins, H. (1988). *Star Trek* rerun, reread, rewritten: Fan writing as textual poaching. *Critical Studies in Mass Communication*, 5(2), pp. 85–107.

Jenkins, H. (1992). *Textual Poachers: Television Fans and Participatory Culture*. London: Routledge.

Jenkins, H. (2008). *Convergence Culture: Where Old and New Media Collide*. New York: New York University Press.

Jenkins, H. (2011a). "Cultural acupuncture": Fan activism and the Harry Potter Alliance. *Transformative Works and Cultures*, 10. https://doi.org /10.3983/twc.2012.0305

Jenkins, H. (2011b, June 24). Three reasons why Pottermore matters: Confessions of an AcaFan. http://henryjenkins.org/blog/2011/06/three_reasons_why_pottermore_m.html

Jenkins, H. (2012). *Textual Poachers: Television Fans and Participatory Culture: Updated Twentieth Anniversary Edition*. New York and London: Routledge.

Jennette, A. (2013, September 29). Defining the "Harry Potter" generation. Mugglenet.com. www.mugglenet.com/2013/09/defining-the-harry-potter-generation/

jkrowling.com (2018). Terms of use. www.jkrowling.com/tcs/

Jones, N., Rundell, K., McNally, R., & Chakrabati, S. (2017, November 23). The Harry Potter effect: A discussion on how the Harry Potter books have changed the landscape of children's literature and permeated our cultural consciousness [recording of panel discussion]. Royal Society of Literature. https://rsliterature.org/library-article/the-harry-potter-effect/

Jones, P. (2012, March 28). How Pottermore cast an ebook spell over Amazon. *The Guardian*. www.theguardian.com/books/booksblog/2012/mar/28/pottermore-ebook-amazon-harry-potter

Jones, P. (2015, September 10). Pottermore readies radical relaunch. *The Bookseller*. www.thebookseller.com/news/pottermore-readies-radical-relaunch-312036

Just, J. (2010, April 1). The parent problem in young adult lit. *New York Times*. www.nytimes.com/2010/04/04/books/review/Just-t.html?pagewanted=all

Kent Potterfest 2017 (2017). www.facebook.com/events/376920692675541/?active_tab=discussion [link was broken as of May 2018].

Kettering, S. (2017). Kent Potterfest 2017. Facebook group. www.facebook.com/events/376920692675541/?active_tab=discussion

Larsen, K. (2015). (Re)Claiming Harry Potter fan pilgrimage sites. In L. S. Brenner, ed., *Playing Harry Potter: Essays and Interviews on Fandom and Performance*. Jefferson, NC: McFarland.

Liao, S. (2017, December 12). This Harry Potter AI-generated fanfiction is remarkably good. The Verge.com. www.theverge.com/2017/12/12/16768582/harrypotter-ai-fanfiction

Little Studio Big Art (2013). Harry Potter festival. www.littlestudiobigart.com/harry-potter-fest

Loot Crate (2018). J. K. Rowling's wizarding world. www.lootcrate.com/crates/wizarding-world

Main Street Kent (n.d.). About. http://mainstreetkent.org/about/

Marantz, A. (2015). The virologist: How a young entrepreneur built an empire by repackaging memes. *New Yorker*. www.newyorker.com/magazine/2015/01/05/virologist

Martens, M. (2016). *Publishers, Readers, and Digital Engagement*. London: Palgrave Macmillan.

Marwick, A., & boyd, d. (2011). To see and be seen: Celebrity practice on Twitter. *Convergence*, 17(2), pp. 139–58. https://doi.org/10.1177/1354856510394539

McGrath, C. (2005, November 13). The Narnia skirmishes. *New York Times*. www.nytimes.com/2005/11/13/movies/the-narnia-skirmishes.html

Meadows, S. (2017). Kent Potterfest 2017 Facebook group post. www.facebook.com/events/376920692675541/?active_tab=discussion

Menta, A. (2017, December 14). Absurd new "Harry Potter" book written by predictive text already has fan art. *Newsweek*. www.newsweek.com/new-harry-potter-book-written-predictive-text-already-has-fan-art-748331

Merriam-Webster (2018). Pilgrimage. www.merriam-webster.com/dictionary/pilgrimage

Miller, L. (2018, March 16). Teens already know how to overthrow the government. *The Cut*. www.thecut.com/2018/03/parkland-students-emma-gonzalez-david-hogg.html

Mills, A. (2016). Colonialism in wizarding America: JK Rowling's history of magic in North America through an Indigenous lens. *The Looking Glass: New Perspectives on Children's Literature*, 19(1). www.the-looking-glass.net/index.php/tlg/article/view/764/709

Moran, J. (2000). *Star Authors: Literary Celebrity in America*. Sterling, VA: Pluto Press.

Murray, S. (2004). "Celebrating the story the way it is": Cultural studies, corporate media and the contested utility of fandom. *Continuum*, 18(1), pp. 7–25. https://doi.org/10.1080/1030431032000180978

Murray, S., & Weber, M. (2017). "Live and local"? The significance of digital media for writers' festivals. *Convergence: The International Journal of New Media Technologies*, 23(1), pp. 61–78.

New York Times (2017, 24 September). Children's series [section of 'Best Sellers' listing]. *The New York Times*. www.nytimes.com/books/best-sellers/2017/09/24/series-books/?action=click&contentCollection=Books&referrer=https%3A%2F%2Fwww.google.com%2F&region=Header&module=ArrowNav&version=Right&pgtype=Reference

Nicolas, A. (2018). Formes de représentation, impératif d'actualité et enjeux de pouvoir sur les dispositifs numériques: L'Exemple de J. K. Rowling et du site. *Mémoires du livre*, 9(2), https://doi.org/10.7202/1046986ar

O Hayes [@ohaaayes]. (2018, April 21). "How on earth … ". Twitter. https://twitter.com/search?f=tweets&q=there%20was%20a%20Jewish%20guy%20at%2Howarts%E2%80%9D%20is%20not%20representation.%20Neither%20was%20decidin%20Dumbledore%20was%20gay%20&src=typd.

OhioFestivals.net (2017, July 29). Kent Potterfest review. https://ohiofestivals.net/potterfest/

Ohlsson, A., Forslid, T., & Steiner, A. (2014). Literary celebrity reconsidered. *Celebrity Studies*, 5(1–2), pp. 32–44.

Ommundsen, W. (2004). Sex, soap and sainthood: Beginning to theorise literary celebrity. *Journal of the Association for the Study of Australian Literature*, 3, 45–56.

Ommundsen, W. (2009). Literary festivals and cultural consumption. *Australian Literary Studies*, 24(1), pp. 19–34.

Oxford University Press (2018). Slacktivism. *Oxford Living Dictionary*. https://en.oxforddictionaries.com/definition/slacktivism

Pearson, R. (2010). Fandom in the digital era. *Popular Communication*, 8(1), pp. 84–95. https://doi.org/10.1080/15405700903502346

Pew Research Center (2018, March 1). Defining generations: Where millennials end and postmillennials begin. www.pewresearch.org/fact-tank/2018/03/01/defining-generations-where-millennials-end-and-post-millennials-begin/

Plante, C. N., Roberts, S. E., Reysen, S., & Gerbasi, K. C. (2014). "One of us": Engagement with fandoms and global citizenship identification. *Psychology of Popular Media Culture*, 3(1), pp. 49–64. https://doi.org/10.1037/ppm0000008

Pollock, A. [@alainapol22]. (2018, April 24). Should i change my twitter profile to "J K. Rowling liked my tweet". Am i basically famous now????? Twitter. https://twitter.com/search?q=Should%20i%20change%20my%20twitter%20profile%20to%20%E2%80%9CJ%20K.%20Rowling%20liked%20my%20tweet%E2%80%9D.%20Am%20i%20basically%20famous%20now&src=typd

Prendergast, L. (2017). Harry Potter and the Millennial mind: How J.K. Rowling shaped the political thinking of a generation. *The Spectator*. www.spectator.co.uk/2017/06/harry-potter-and-the-millenial-mind/

Propp, V. (1968). *Morphology of the Folktale*, 2nd edn. Austin, TX, and London: University of Texas Press.

Pugh, T., & Wallace, D. L. (2006). Heteronormative heroism and queering the school story in JK Rowling's Harry Potter series. *Children's Literature Association Quarterly*, 31(3), p. 268.

Pugh, T., & Wallace, D. L. (2008). A postscript to "Heteronormative heroism and queering the school story in JK Rowling's Harry Potter series." *Children's Literature Association Quarterly*, 33(2), pp. 188–92.

Recuero, R., Amaral, A., & Monteiro, C. (2012). Fandoms, trending topics and social capital in Twitter. *AoIR Selected Papers of Internet Research*, 2. https://journals.uic.edu/ojs/index.php/spir/article/view/8217

Respers France, L. (2018, February 2). J. K. Rowling responds to gay Dumbledore controversy. CNN Entertainment. www.cnn.com/2018/02/01/entertainment/jk-rowling-dumbledore-gay/index.html

Roanoke Harry Potter Festival (n.d.). www.roanokepotterfest.com/meet-us/

Rose, F. (2011, July 20). Magic indeed: J. K. Rowling rethinks the art of fiction. *Wired Magazine*. www.wired.com/2011/07/rowling-rethinks-art-fiction/

Rowling, J. K. (n.d.). Ilvermorny School of Witchcraft and Wizardry. Pottermore. www.pottermore.com/writing-by-jk-rowling/ilvermorny

Rowling, J. K. (1998). *Harry Potter and the Sorcerer's Stone*. New York: Scholastic.

Ruddock, A. (2001). *Understanding Audiences*. London: SAGE.

Ruddock, A. (2007). *Investigating Audiences*. London: SAGE.

Schäfer, M. (2015). Digital public sphere. In G. Mazzoleni et al., eds., *International Encyclopedia of Political Communication*. London: Wiley, pp. 322–8.

Serjeant, J. (2007, October 15). J. K. Rowling launches U.S. book tour with mass signing. Reuters. www.reuters.com/article/us-usa-rowling/j-k-rowling-launches-u-s-book-tour-with-mass-signing-idUSN1537267520071015

Sims, D. (2015, September 18). In defense of Hufflepuff. *The Atlantic*. www
.theatlantic.com/entertainment/archive/2015/09/hufflepuff-rules
/405937/

Sklar, R. (2018, March 26). Harry Potter inspired the Parkland generation.
CNN. www.cnn.com/2018/03/26/opinions/parkland-march-harry-
potter-generation-opinion-sklar/index.html

Smith, D. (2017, August 1). Potterfest summons throngs to Kent. *Record
Courier*.

Stephenson, A. (2016). *The Construction of Authorship and Audience in the
Production and Consumption of Children's Film Adaptations*. Unpublished
PhD dissertation, University of Southampton.

Stevie Weevie D [@Stoxen42] (2016, May 26), I took the Pottermore test
and good news! Twitter. https://twitter.com/search?q=I%20took%
20the%20Pottermore%20test%20and%20good%20news!%20I%27m%20a
%20Hufflepuff%20too!%20%20%20Oh%20wait%20that%27s%20horrible
%20news%20Damnit.&src=typd

Stiefvater, M. (2018). About. Tumblr. http://maggie-stiefvater.tumblr.com
/about

Swinehart, K.R. (2017). Kent Potterfest 2017 Facebook group post. www
.facebook.com/events/376920692675541/?active_tab=discussion

Terranova, T. (2000). Free labor: Producing culture for the digital
economy. *Social Text*, 63, pp. 33–57.

The Guardian Data Blog (2016, August 9). The top 100 bestselling books of
all time: How does Fifty Shades of Grey compare? www.theguardian.com
/news/datablog/2012/aug/09/best-selling-books-all-time-fifty-shades-
grey-compare

Thérenty, M. E., & Wrona, A. (2013, 14 June). L'Écrivain comme marque:
Agenda. [The author as a brand: Agenda]. Conference program. www
.fabula.org/actualites/l-ecrivain-comme-marque_57463.php

Thérenty, M. E., & Wrona, A., eds. (2018). *L'Écrivain comme marque*. [The author as a brand]. Paris: Presses universitaires de la Sorbonne.

Tosenberger, C. (2008). Homosexuality at the online Hogwarts: Harry Potter slash fanfiction. *Children's Literature*, 36(1), pp. 185–207.

Twitter Help (n.d.). Parody, commentary, and fan account policy. https://help.twitter.com/articles/106373?lang=en

Universal Theme Park Orlando (2018). The Wizarding World of Harry Potter. www.universalorlando.com/web/en/us/things-to-do/rides-attractions/harry-potter-and-the-escape-from-gringotts/index.html

Urban Dictionary (n.d.). Fanon. www.urbandictionary.com/define.php?term=Fanon

Vander Ark, S. (2004, July 1). Fan site award. The Harry Potter Lexicon. www.hp-lexicon.org/author/steve-vanderark/

Vickers, A. (2001, January 22). Warner Bros. in fresh battle over Harry Potter website. *The Guardian*. www.theguardian.com/media/2001/jan/22/newmedia1

visitphilly.com (n.d.). Witches & Wizards Festival. www.visitphilly.com/events/philadelphia/harry-potter-weekend-in-chestnut-hill/

Vlogbrothers [podcast] (n.d.). Featured. www.youtube.com/user/vlogbrothers/featured

Waldman, K. (2014, March 21). Everyone knows where they belong. *Slate*. www.slate.com/articles/arts/culturebox/2014/03/divergent_harry_potter_and_ya_fiction_s_desire_for_self_categorization.html

Walter, N. (2004, October 26). Works in progress. *The Guardian*. www.theguardian.com/books/2004/oct/27/technology.news

Walton, S. S. (2018). The leaky canon: Constructing and policing heteronormativity in the Harry Potter fandom. *Journal of Audience & Reception Studies*, 15(1), pp. 231–51.

Weber, M. (2014). Conceptualizing audience experience at the literary festival. *Continuum: Journal of Media & Cultural Studies*, 29(1), pp. 84–96. https://doi.org/10.1080/10304312.2014.986058

Weber, M. (2018). *Literary Festivals and Contemporary Book Culture*. London: Palgrave Macmillan.

Weiss, J. (2018, February 2). Harry Potter becomes best-selling book series in history with more than 500 million copies sold worldwide. *Syfy Wire*. www.syfy.com/syfywire/harry-potter-becomes-best-selling-book-series -in-history-with-more-than-500-million-copies

Williams, R. (1983). *Keywords: A Vocabulary of Culture and Society*, rev. edn. New York: Oxford University Press.

Wyatt, D. (2015, July 31). Why Harry Potter's aged 35, not 26. *The Independent*. www.independent.co.uk/arts-entertainment/books/ news/why-harry-potters-aged-35 not-26–10430209.html

Young Lee, P. (2016, July 1). Pottermore problems: Scholars and writers call foul on J. K. Rowling's North American magic. *Salon*. www .salon.com/2016/07/01/pottermore_problems_scholars_and_writers_ call_foul_on_j_k_rowlings_north_american_magic/

Zoellner, A. (2017, April 4). Fans, vendors updated on Potter Fest. *Daily Union*. www.dailyunion.com/news/article_fef6b16e-2121-11e7-b583-3769de21fe58.html

Acknowledgments

Thanks to Melanie Ramdarshan-Bold, whose vision created the idea for this Element, to graduate assistants Morgan Messenheimer and Jacquie Kociubuk for their diligent research assistance, and to the peer reviewers, whose thoughtful comments and expert criticism greatly improved the manuscript. Thanks also to Kate Epstein and her editorial team and to Dave Morris and Lucy Metzger at Cambridge University Press.

I am grateful for support from the Research and Creative Activity Fund at Kent State's College of Communication and Information (Drs. Amy Reynolds, Danielle Coombs, Kendra Albright, and Ms. Audrey Lingenfelter and A. J. Leu), and a fellowship from Bournemouth University's School of Journalism, English, and Communication, which subsidized this project.

Thanks to my husband Carlos for his endless support, and to Alexander and Christian who first got me interested in *Harry Potter*, and who give meaning to my life on a daily basis. Thanks also to my personal cheerleaders: Alis, Helle, Carl, and Barbara. I am grateful for you always. Thanks to all who agreed to be interviewed about their *Harry Potter* fandom, and to those who have permitted me to use their social media quotes in this text.

Cambridge Elements

Publishing and Book Culture

SERIES EDITOR

Samantha Rayner
University College London

Samantha Rayner is a Reader in UCL's Department of Information Studies. She is also Director of UCL's Centre for Publishing, co-Director of the Bloomsbury CHAPTER (Communication History, Authorship, Publishing, Textual Editing and Reading) and co-editor of the Academic Book of the Future BOOC (Book as Open Online Content) with UCL Press.

ASSOCIATE EDITOR

Rebecca Lyons
University of Bristol

Rebecca Lyons is a Teaching Fellow at the University of Bristol. She is also co-editor of the experimental BOOC (Book as Open Online Content) at UCL Press. She teaches and researches book and reading history, particularly female owners and readers of Arthurian literature in fifteenth- and sixteenth-century England, and also has research interests in digital academic publishing.

About the Series

This series aims to fill the demand for easily accessible, quality texts available for teaching and research in the diverse and dynamic fields of Publishing and Book Culture. Rigorously researched and peer-reviewed Elements will be published under themes, or 'Gatherings'. These Elements should be the first check point for researchers or students working on that area of publishing and book trade history and practice: we hope that, situated so logically at Cambridge University Press, where academic publishing in the UK began, the series will develop to create an unrivalled space where these histories and practices can be investigated and preserved.

Cambridge Elements

Publishing and Book Culture Young Adult Publishing

Gathering Editor: Melanie Ramdarshan Bold
Melanie Ramdarshan Bold is Associate Professor at University College
London. Her main research interest centers on contemporary authorship,
publishing, and reading, with a focus on books for children and young
adults. She is the author of *Inclusive Young Adult Fiction: Authors of Colour in
the United Kingdom* (2018).

ELEMENTS IN THE GATHERING

Young People, Comics and Reading: Exploring a Complex Reading Experience
Lucia Cedeira Serantes

*The Forever Fandom of Harry Potter: Balancing
Fan Agency and Corporate Control*
Marianne Martens

A full series listing is available at: www.cambridge.org/EPBC

CPSIA information can be obtained
at www.ICGtesting.com
Printed in the USA
LVHW080857150719
624101LV00010B/143/P

9 781108 469883